Always Home

50 YEARS OF THE USO

Always Home

THE OFFICIAL PHOTOGRAPHIC HISTORY

By Frank Coffey

Special Foreword by Bob Hope

BRASSEY'S (US), Inc.
A Division of Maxwell Macmillan, Inc.

Washington • New York • London • Oxford
Beijing • Frankfurt • São Paulo • Sydney • Tokyo • Toronto

Brassey's (US), Inc.

Editorial Offices	Order Department
Brassey's (US), Inc.	Brassey's Book Orders
8000 Westpark Drive	c/o Macmillan Publishing Co.
First Floor	100 Front Street, Box 500
McLean, Virginia 22102	Riverside, New Jersey 08075

Brassey's (US), Inc., books are available at special discounts for bulk purchases
for sales promotions, premiums, fund-raising, or educational use through the
Special Sales Director, Macmillan Publishing Company, 866 Third Avenue,
New York, New York 10022.

Library of Congress Cataloging-in-Publication Data
Coffey, Frank.
Always home: 50 years of the USO—the official photographic
history/by Frank Coffey: foreword by Chapman B. Cox.
p.   cm.
ISBN 0-08-040576-2
1. United Service Organizations (U.S.) I. Title
UH905.C64 1991
355.1'2'06073—dc20   91-6870
CIP

British Library Cataloguing in Publication Data
Coffey, Frank
Always home: 50 years of the USO: the official photographic history.
1. United States. Military forces. Welfare services.
History
I. Title
355.340973

ISBN 0-08-040576-2

10 9 8 7 6 5 4 3 2 1

Published in the United States of America

The
only thing necessary
for the triumph
of evil
is for good men
to do
nothing.

This book is dedicated to those who served.

Contents

Special Foreword

On February 4 the USO (United Service Organizations) celebrated its fiftieth anniversary of serving our nation's servicemen and servicewomen at home and overseas, during peacetime and during war. And in May 1991, I'll be celebrating my fifty-year relationship with the USO. Few marriages last that long, and what's more, we've never said a harsh word to one another.

However, the thought crossed my mind that the USO is not the greatest booking agent in the world. How many people actually know where Goose Bay, Keflavik, Thule, Torrejon, Diego Garcia, and most recently, East Dhahran are? I didn't know they even existed until the USO booked me there. Happily, when the USO planned my visits, it made sure they were round trips.

Thanks to the USO, my knowledge of geography has been greatly enhanced. And I have some wonderful memories—like box lunches, yellow fever shots—and I've learned to say "Kaopectate" in nine languages. Hey, the USO has given me things that will stay with me the rest of my life . . . so my doctor tells me.

But I'm not complaining. How else would I get to travel with Carroll Baker, Jill St. John, Lana Turner, Ann-Margret, and Raquel Welch and have my wife wish me "bon voyage"?

It should be noted that the USO is a civilian organization entirely dedicated to working with our military. It operates solely by civilian volunteers, is administered by a civilian staff, and is devoted to the off-duty needs of U.S. military forces.

The fact that it doesn't depend upon tax money for support may be the reason why the planes the USO provided were not always the greatest. The first year, they gave me a plane that belonged to a four-star general—Pershing. I knew the plane was old when I saw the pilot sitting behind me wearing goggles and a scarf. When they rolled the steps away, the plane fell over on its side.

For a long time with the USO I didn't know if I was an entertainer or a test pilot. Come on, some of the planes were even turned down by kamikaze pilots.

The USO began in 1941 as the Hollywood community rallied to bring entertainment to our troops, stateside and abroad. With the outbreak of World War II, the organization more than tripled its efforts to provide the military with a "pause" from both the terror and tedium of war.

The USO show of World War II conjures up the image of a comedian and musicians on a makeshift stage surrounded by thousands of GIs and a singer belting out the saga of "Boogie Woogie Bugle Boy of Company B."

Historically, the USO has had its ups-and-downs. Following 1948, the organization was virtually out of business. But three years later, with the Korean conflict, the USO came back strong. Thereafter, renewed organizational energies came during Vietnam. With the Vietnam evacuation in 1973, activities lessened again. But the USO continued to serve our men and women in uniform and extended its services to include their dependents.

Today, in the Middle East, "Boogie Woogie Bugle Boy" has been replaced by "Jump"; and because of security, audiences may be smaller, and large stage productions have given way to a handshake, a joke, and a simple song. Two constants remain: the USO makes sure that the "show goes on!"; and the audiences are still the greatest in the world. When they laugh, they mean it; when they applaud, there just isn't any better sound in the world.

The audiences truly appreciate the USO and the performers. When they look up on that stage they see home, family. . . . They see America.

For fifty years, the USO has brought solace and comfort and laughter to millions of GIs all around the globe. There isn't one GI whose spirits haven't been lifted and loneliness relieved for an hour or two by the talented and dedicated gypsies sent out by the USO.

For fifty years, I've seen the USO bring an oasis of America to our men and women overseas, and I've watched the magic of a cup of coffee, a game of pool, a video game, and a friendly face boost morale.

Currently in the Middle East, our men and women in uniform stand in the twilight between civilization and the raw savagery of war. It is inconceivable that they be asked to serve without some touchstone of our sympathy and support. The USO is that touchstone.

I welcome this opportunity to salute the wonderful people whose tireless efforts have made the USO such a vital part of our society. From the performers who unselfishly give their time and talents to entertain at our military bases to the volunteer serving coffee and sandwiches at local USO facilities here at home and to those individuals who generously provide financial support for the organization, I say, "Thanks for a job well done."

Bob Hope

Foreword

In this volume we were given the challenge to retrace the people, events, and forces that combined to propel the United Service Organizations (USO) to this point — "50 Years' Service to Service People."

Literally millions have volunteered over the years — as entertainers, board members, fundraisers, hosts and hostesses, club and snack bar attendants — all leaving their own unique imprint on the USO's heritage. Their personal energy has kept the USO vibrant and alive.

Millions have also contributed financially and have given even more when times have been tough. And so many corporations — from small family businesses to international giants — have shared their collective expertise and financial resources in times of war and peace since 1941.

So many have given so much that it would be impossible to cover it all, so we have tried rather to capture the flavor of the USO through pictures and a brief chronology of its past. Some individuals are named, some specific events are recounted, but many more are not. A few memorable quotes and a lot of great photos are here for your enjoyment. Beyond that, we want to say to all who have ever been involved — thank you.

The USO would also like to acknowledge Teri Tynes, Ray Volpe, and Frank Weimann for their efforts in making this possible, as well as the members of the USO fiftieth anniversary task force, the Armed Forces Professional Entertainment Office (AFPO), and all the photographers whose works appear here. The words "always home" convey what the USO has meant to the American people and our servicemen, servicewomen, and their families through three wars and the peacetimes in between.

As you will read in the pages ahead, this organization was founded to address the needs of an exploding military population that was taxing the resources of communities across the country, communities with few outlets for recreation or other off-duty morale programs.

Something had to be done and quickly. National leaders called upon members of the business, entertainment, and civic communities — and ultimately the American people — to figure out what. As the United States prepared for potential involvement in an escalating world war, the birth of the USO represented the civilian response to that need.

In no other country in the world could such an organization have so profound an impact on so many. The American spirit of volunteerism remains unparalleled, and it is that spirit that has ensured the health of the USO for half a century. Today this same spirit is shown by the citizens of Japan, Korea, the Philippines, Germany, Italy, Israel, France, Bahrain, the United Arab Emirates, and Iceland, all of whom now host USO facilities on their soil. As the USO has evolved over the years, many other countries have hosted us as well.

Founded on February 4, 1941, the USO now celebrates its fiftieth anniversary in the midst of another crisis with dramatic worldwide implications. As this manuscript is delivered to the publisher, the United States — indeed the world community — is in the midst of war in the Persian Gulf. The invasion of Kuwait by Iraqi forces on August 2, 1990, presented the world with its first serious post–cold war predicament. And it thrust the USO into the limelight once again, to react immediately to a crisis situation.

To those who comprise the USO today, these stark events remind us that we must always be ready. This nation must be prepared to defend the principles of democracy and freedom. The USO must remain able to respond to national military crises, while at the same time continue to provide our customary services to military personnel and their families every single day of the year.

We hope that you enjoy this brief journey through the USO's five decades of service. Perhaps for you it will be a "trip down memory lane." You may have been part of a tremendous international effort to make sure the USO is "always home."

Chapman B. Cox
President, World USO

Acknowledgments

I wish to thank Brassey's editor Don McKeon, a fellow baseball fan-atic, for his astute management of a complex project; and Vicki Chamlee, Brassey's able production manager, for carefully shepherding the book home. At the USO, Kevin McCarthy provided important eleventh-hour help. Most of all, I would like to express my sincere appreciation to the organization's manager of publications and information, Amy Adler, for her professionalism, tireless effort, and indefatigable good cheer.

I would also like to express my appreciation to Yaron Fidler, the book's multitalented designer, for bringing *Always Home* so vividly and dramatically to life.

Thanks also go to Allen Wexler for his astute editorial contributions and to Carl Waldman, John Rumsey, Jr., John Palmer, and Wayne Coffey for their friendship and support. Also, a most sincere tip of the hat to Frank Weimann, agent extraordinaire and friend. And finally my gratitude to my father, Lt. Col. Frank B. Coffey, USAF (ret.).

Chapter 1

The Beginning of the USO

In the spring of 1940, what had been known as the "phony war" in Europe erupted into a real, full-blown, shooting conflict. It was the beginning of a nightmare that would engulf the world. Hitler's armies overran Denmark, Norway, Belgium, and Luxembourg; by June, they had swept around the Maginot line and across France, and driven the British Army off the Continent at Dunkirk.

As Europe fell under the shadow of Nazi aggression, and Asia came under the heel of the expansionist Japanese Empire, America reluctantly readied itself for a war that was rapidly engulfing the world. The United States responded to the impending global conflict with the enactment of the Selective Service and Training Act of 1940, planning initially to induct nine hundred thousand men into the armed forces for a period of up to twelve months, a term that soon afterward was extended to eighteen months.

As the first peacetime draft in U.S. history, this sudden mobilization of such a large number of young men immediately created severe social problems. Near small towns all across the country, military training camps seemed to spring up overnight. They were soon filled with thousands of newly inducted young men from all walks of life and from all parts of the country, most of them far from home and all that was familiar to them for the first time in their lives.

You see them near forts and camps spread out along the highways in dejected groups eager for sport and civilian contact, with none to be had. You find them clustered in bewildered and uncertain knots on street corners in tiny towns overrun with their kind, or lined up in patient queues outside small town movie houses.

So wrote Meyer Berger of the *New York Times* in a May 1941 article commenting on the impact of rapid mobilization on small-town America. The isolationist sentiments of the 1920s and 1930s were still very much alive as America's entry into World War II loomed. Small communities across the nation reacted with skeptical reserve, and sometimes alarm, at the sudden influx of these legions of strangers, fearing, too, the appearance of the worst elements of corruption and vice often found across military installations.

Nor were things any better from the point of view of those early inductees. The small towns near the training camps offered little in the way of off-duty recreation, and besides, on a soldier's pay, there was not much an enlisted man could afford to do anyway.

The United States had always relied on an army of citizen-soldiers in times of dire national emergencies. As George Washington once noted, "When we assumed the soldier, we did not lay aside the citizen."

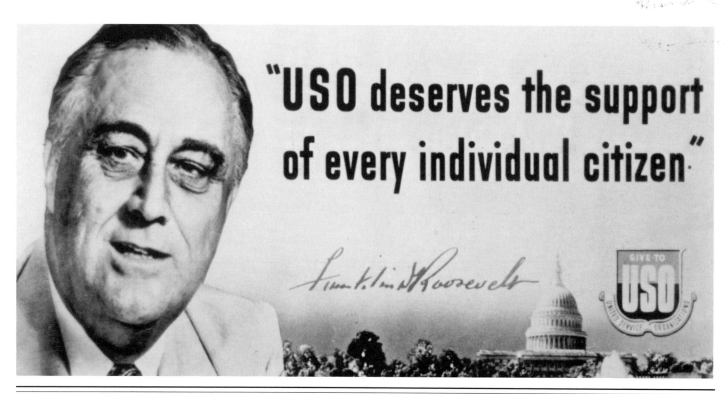

The USO's first honorary chairman, Franklin D. Roosevelt, was also one of its first "poster boys."

The tradition of civilian support for America's fighting men dates back to the Revolutionary War and Mary Hays, whose efforts to bring water to her husband and other American patriot soldiers in the Battle of Monmouth in 1778 immortalized her as "Molly Pitcher."

During the Civil War, in 1862, at the Battle of Fredericksburg, a charitable group served Union troops hot coffee from wagons brought to the edge of the northern Virginia battlefield. In World War I, entertainer Elsie Janis — virtually the only "name" performer to do so — abandoned her stage career in New York City and dedicated herself to entertaining American troops on the front lines in France.

In 1940, with America facing the greatest challenge to its survival as a free society, steps again had to be taken to ensure the morale and welfare of the young men, and increasing numbers of young women, who had been committed to defend the nation. In addition, the problems of hundreds of small towns across America, suddenly finding themselves ill prepared to act as hosts for hundreds of thousands of American servicemen and women, had to be addressed.

A number of private agencies had provided comfort and social services to American troops in France toward the close of World War I in 1918. Representatives of these organizations were called together in New York City in October 1940 for the first of a series of meetings hosted by Frank Weil of the National Jewish Welfare Board to discuss what should be done.

Meanwhile, the federal government had also become concerned with maintaining morale among the troops and with offsetting the negative impact the mobilization was having on local communities. Although both the Federal Security Agency and the War Department wanted the morale effort to be under direct government control, President Franklin Delano Roosevelt believed that what was most needed was a way to keep service personnel in touch with the civilian life, a life that nearly all of them had recently left behind so abruptly.

Six of the organizations that Frank Weil had brought together in New York — the Young Women's Christian Association (YWCA), the Young Men's Christian Association (YMCA), National Catholic Community Service, the National Jewish Welfare Board, the Traveler's Aid Association, and the Salvation Army — pooled their resources to form the United Service Organizations for National Defense, later shortened to the United Service Organizations (USO). New York City department store executive and Salvation Army director Walter Hoving was appointed its first president, and Thomas E. Dewey, the future governor of New York, headed its initial fund-raising drive.

In January 1941 Roosevelt summoned the USO leaders to Washington, D.C., where a meeting was held with Paul McNutt, director of the Federal Security Agency; Adm. Chester Nimitz, chief of naval operations; Gen. George Marshall, Army chief of staff; and Mrs. Frederick Osborn, chairman of the Joint Army and Navy Committee on Welfare and Recreation. When a stalemate developed over what areas would fall under civilian or military control, Roosevelt himself broke the deadlock with this pointed directive:

> This is the way I want it done! I want these private organizations to handle the on-leave recreation of the men in the armed forces. The government should put up the buildings and some name common to the organization should appear on the outside.

And so, as the nation's inevitable entry into the war approached, the USO was born.

Three servicemen — happy, relaxed, cared for. In these faces the USO's mission can be plainly seen.

Chapter 2

The USO in World War II: A Home Away from Home

On February 4, 1941, the USO was incorporated in New York State, and by the end of its first year of operation under the financial leadership of National Campaign chairman Thomas Dewey, it had raised over $16 million. In 1942 Dewey resigned to run for the governorship of New York (he won) and was replaced as chairman by Prescott Bush, then a partner with Brown Brothers Harriman & Co. and later a U.S. senator from Connecticut. Bush, who also was chairman of the National War Fund, contributed mightily to the $33 million raised by the USO during World War II. (History will also note another important contribution from Chairman Bush: his son George would become the forty-first president of the United States.)

With a solid financial base, USO centers began to appear all over the country not only near training centers, but also at bus and railroad terminals to serve the needs of soldiers in transit.

The first USO centers were established in various locations, including railroad sleeping cars, barns, museums, and churches. On November 28, 1941, the first permanent government-built USO center opened in Fayetteville, North Carolina, for the soldiers at nearby Fort Bragg. USO facilities sprang up in towns across the nation as community spirit rose to meet the challenges brought on by military mobilization. Some of them—like the USO centers in San Jose, California, and Wendover Field, Utah

—sprouted up literally overnight, built in one day with material and labor donated by local residents.

During the next five years, like shining beacons of light from home, USO clubs operated at over three thousand locations, both stateside and around the world, providing a "time out" from the war for over twelve million men and women in uniform. Without indulging in hyperbole, it can be safely said that the USO's effort was nothing short of herculean and its impact monumentally important to the nation's war effort.

USO centers were intended to provide armed forces personnel with a "home away from home," a place where a soldier could spend time outside of a strictly military atmosphere. Young women from the local community volunteered as hostesses, providing civilian contact at dances, parties, and other social activities.

There were no rigid guidelines for the way in which the individual USO centers operated. Instead, each one adapted to the particular needs of the military communities it served. Most provided facilities for sewing on insignias, washing up, and writing letters home as well as lounges for meeting with friends or for taking a nap while waiting for a train or bus. Travel and sightseeing information was made available to soldiers in transit, along with a check room. Local clergymen provided religious or other personal counseling for soldiers far from home.

Although these basic services could be found at

almost every USO facility, each center and club developed a unique character that reflected the civilian community from which its staffers were drawn. In Honolulu, for example, the USO center became famous for its banana splits. ("My Lord!" one GI exclaimed. "Those splits were what made life worth living!") At the peak of its operation, the center was using nearly a ton of bananas and 250 gallons of ice cream each day to meet the demand of the millions of service personnel on their way to and from the war zones in the South Pacific.

The biggest concentration of USO centers during World War II was in the Hawaiian islands. There, after the Japanese attack on Pearl Harbor on December 7, 1941, U.S. territory had become a war zone overnight. Thousands of troops began to pour into the islands.

Local young women who had volunteered as USO hostesses formed what became known as the Flying Squadron. One of its original members, Mrs. Frances Hurd Buxton of Alameda, California, recalls:

> [I] was a member of the USO Flying Squadron which was composed of young business girls in Honolulu, Hawaii. We went to the various service posts to dance with the enlisted personnel. We were organized in 1942 and the dances were held on Sunday afternoons. These dances were so popular that before long the officers asked if the Flying Squadron wouldn't also come to their dances.
>
> One very memorable event was attending a dance at a Marine cantonment in honor of Major James Roosevelt, USMC, and dancing a dance with him. Another thing I remembered with pleasure was dancing a polka with a sailor when soon everyone left the dance floor to watch and applaud us.
>
> Besides going to these dances, groups of three girls would go with an officer to visit the boys in various outposts and to take them cookies and magazines. We would always have lunch at one of the posts. We did this every now and then. I certainly enjoyed all these activities, and I'm sure the men did also. I have my USO bracelet, pin and wings, also a very pretty flowered bracelet given at one of the dances. [But] I don't remember why we were called the Flying Squadron—none of us flew.

Stateside, the entry of the United States into the war in December 1941 brought a dramatic change to USO operations. Volunteers in mobile units brought the USO to military personnel stationed on guard duty at sites that did not provide recreational opportunities. With the war effort in full gear by mid-1942, the USO extended its social programs to include not only men and women in uniform, but also the hundreds of thousands of workers in defense plants across the nation who had been relocated to distant communities. For women defense workers with small children and with husbands who were away from home in the armed forces, the USO provided some of the country's first-ever day-care services, such as at Sidney, Nebraska, where hundreds of children were cared for.

The great buildup in troop strength after Pearl Harbor, with inductees committed to military service for the duration of the war, brought the number of Americans in uniform from nine hundred thousand to twelve million by the war's end. Transportation facilities throughout the country were choked with great masses of soldiers coming from and going to duty assignments.

A main military transit point—the town of Sayre, Pennsylvania, with a population of about seven thousand—was a case in point. One day early in the war, Sayre's USO volunteers, notified that three troop trains were scheduled to stop in the small town, arranged to provide food and hospitality for the soldiers. Much to everyone's surprise, not three, but seven trains filled with troops stopped in Sayre that day, and, remarkably, by four o'clock the following morning, USO volunteers had fed over thirty thousand men, using up the last loaf of bread, bottle of Coke, and drop of milk the town had.

In return for their tireless efforts, USO volunteers on the home front were richly rewarded with gratifying recollections. Ellen Skaff, who directed the USO club at McAlester, Oklahoma, recalled that her "fondest memories are of the young men and women who gladly served their country with no self-pity and no malice." The same dedication can surely be attributed to Skaff and the thousands of other selfless USO workers.

With its clubs and other activities, the USO not only served the needs of America's men and women in uniform, but also provided an effective means of channeling civilian volunteer efforts. By the war's end in 1945, over 1.5 million Americans had contributed their time to the USO. The Hollywood Canteen was also staffed by no-

WALSH
SECRETARY OF STATE

FRANK S. SHARP
DEPUTY SECRETARY

C/P-11

STATE OF NEW YORK
DEPARTMENT OF STATE
DIVISION OF CORPORATIONS
ALBANY   February 4, 1941

Messrs. Weil, Gotshal & Manges,
New York City.

Dear Sirs:

Certificate of Incorporation of

UNITED SERVICE ORGANIZATIONS FOR NATIONAL DEFENSE, INC.

has been received and filed today as requested.

Fee $42.00 paid.   Filing-----------$40.00
                          Certificate------ 2.00

Yours truly,

MICHAEL F. WALSH

Secretary of State

For $42 the USO was incorporated on February 4, 1941.

tables from the entertainment world. As Jeannette Oden, of Atascadero, California, remembers,

I joined the Hollywood Canteen USO [in 1943], where I served on Sunday afternoons. I tell people that I danced my way through the war. I usually rode a bus and 2 streetcars or 3 buses to get to Hollywood. Sometime, I would first go to a lovely big home in the area where screened-in bunks had been built to accommodate visiting service men on weekend passes. There I spent a couple of hours making up beds before going to the Canteen.

Freddy Martin and his band from the Coconut Grove were regulars at the Canteen. They really gave of their time. There were many other great performers. . . . I remember Dinah Shore and Red Skelton, who seemed to perform more often than many. There were notables of the film world doing kitchen duty, also, and one never saw them out front.

I have a certificate signed by Bette Davis, the actress, who was president of the Hollywood Canteen, thanking me for my services.

Soon after the United States entered the war in 1941, the USO began to step up its programs in stateside military hospitals, which, with tragic inevitability, had begun to fill with wounded and sick military personnel. Volunteers regularly reached out to soldier-patients in hospitals during the most emotionally vulnerable period of their young lives and visited them at a time when they were separated not only from their families at home, but also from their friends in the military. USO workers in hospitals assisted the wounded in writing letters home and provided much-needed companionship. In addition, USO volunteer artists went to the hospitals, where they would sketch portraits of the wounded GIs to send back to their families.

In mid-1942, with the United States fully involved in the war, the USO's first honorary chairman, President Roosevelt, reviewed how his recommendations for the USO morale effort had been carried out: "This is more than we were able to do during the last war. All agencies under one tent. This is a fine job!"

Six months before America's formal entry into the war, Thomas Dewey, national campaign chairman, was busy traveling and speaking on behalf of the USO. On June 6, 1941, Harvey Firestone — a lifelong friend and supporter of the USO — and Dewey (top row, left) spoke in Cleveland, Ohio, as all signs pointed to impending war.

Soldiers, sailors, and marines at Union Station, Washington, D.C., 1942.

Library and music room in the Benedict Club, a Philadelphia USO sponsored by the National Catholic Community Service, 1943.

Union Square, New York, New York. A USO volunteer instructs the troops in the fine art of pigeon feeding.

The USO in World War II: A Home Away from Home **9**

PFC Anthony Yaskulski delivers a check to Ariel Ames, a volunteer worker for the New York USO campaign. The $1,653.24 contribution came from officers, enlisted men, and civilians at Fort Dix, New Jersey.

USO volunteers passing out goodies.

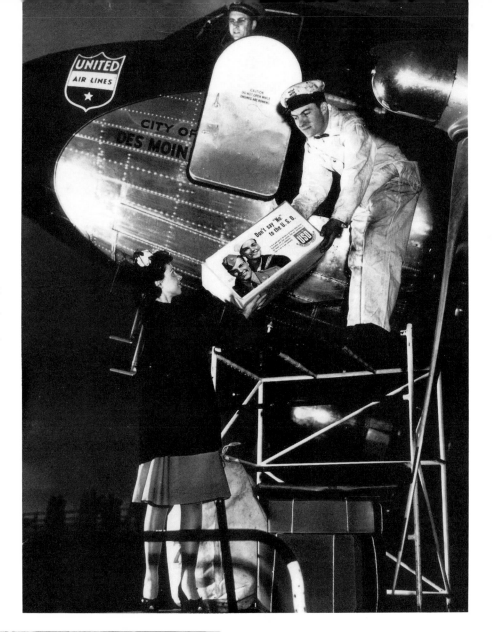

A Des Moines, Iowa, volunteer helping load a USO "care package" destined for a lucky overseas serviceman.

American educator Mary McLeod Bethune, president of the National Council of Negro Women, supervises a game of Chinese checkers for two black soldiers and a host of admirers.

The New York Times.

LATE CITY EDITION
Increasing cloudiness with rising temperature today. Tomorrow cloudy, somewhat colder.
Temperatures Yesterday—Max., 34; Min., 25

Copyright, 1941, by The New York Times Company.

VOL. XCI No. 30,634.

Entered as Second-Class Matter, Postoffice, New York, N. Y.

NEW YORK, MONDAY, DECEMBER 8, 1941.

THREE CENTS NEW YORK CITY and Vicinity

JAPAN WARS ON U. S. AND BRITAIN; MAKES SUDDEN ATTACK ON HAWAII; HEAVY FIGHTING AT SEA REPORTED

CONGRESS DECIDED

Roosevelt Will Address It Today and Find It Ready to Vote War

CONFERENCE IS HELD

Legislative Leaders and Cabinet in Sober White House Talk

By C. P. TRUSSELL
Special to THE NEW YORK TIMES.

WASHINGTON, Dec. 7—President Roosevelt will address a joint session of Congress tomorrow and will find the membership in a mood to vote any steps he asks in connection with the developments in the Pacific.

The President will appear per-

TOKYO ACTS FIRST

Declaration Follows Air and Sea Attacks on U. S. and Britain

TOGO CALLS ENVOYS

After Fighting Is On, Grew Gets Japan's Reply to Hull Note of Nov. 26

By The Associated Press.

TOKYO, Monday, Dec. 8—Japan went to war against the United States and Britain today with air and sea attacks against Hawaii, followed by a formal declaration of hostilities.

Japanese Imperial headquarters announced at 6 A. M. [4 P. M. Sunday, Eastern standard time]

GUAM BOMBED; ARMY SHIP IS SUNK

U. S. Fliers Head North From Manila— Battleship Oklahoma Set Afire by Torpedo Planes at Honolulu

104 SOLDIERS KILLED AT FIELD IN HAWAII

President Fears 'Very Heavy Losses' on Oahu— Churchill Notifies Japan That a State of War Exists

By FRANK L. KLUCKHOHN
Special to THE NEW YORK TIMES.

WASHINGTON, Monday, Dec. 8—Sudden and unexpected attacks on Pearl Harbor, Honolulu, and other United States possessions in the Pacific early yesterday by the Japanese air force and navy plunged the United States and Japan into active war.

The day after Japan's surprise attack on Pearl Harbor the front page of the *New York Times* painted a grim picture.

Ann Sothern, Hedy Lamarr, and Linda Darnell do the honors at the Hollywood Canteen.

USO War Fund Campaign

$32,000,000 for America's Fighting Men, and the Forces Behind the Lines

May 11 — July 4

EMPIRE STATE BLDG., NEW YORK
PENNSYLVANIA 6-5400

March 10, 1942

Mr. Harvey S. Firestone, Jr.
Akron
Ohio

Dear Mr. Firestone:

Mr. Rockefeller and I are delighted to have received your telegram of March 10th accepting our invitation to serve as State Chairman of the USO Campaign Committee in Ohio and as a member of the National Advisory Council.

Your support of this essential part of our country's great national war effort is reassuring and most encouraging. While we feel certain that USO's War Fund Campaign for $32,000,000 will have a strong public appeal, we know that your endorsement of this great endeavor will be extremely helpful in insuring its success.

Thanking you for your telegram, I am

Yours very truly,

Prescott S. Bush
National Campaign Chairman

This letter from Prescott Bush, the USO's second National Campaign chairman, thanked Harvey Firestone for agreeing to help the effort. Bush contributed more than his USO leadership to the war effort: his son George was a decorated Navy pilot in the Pacific theater.

On leave and loving it. Sgt. Franklin Williams with his best girl, Ellen Hardin, in Baltimore, Maryland, 1942.

The handsome USO club in Kauai, Hawaii.

Outside New York's Pennsylvania Station, 1942. A typical and most welcome USO service for men in transit.

The organization's busiest, best-known facility may well have been Honolulu's Army and Navy USO Club.

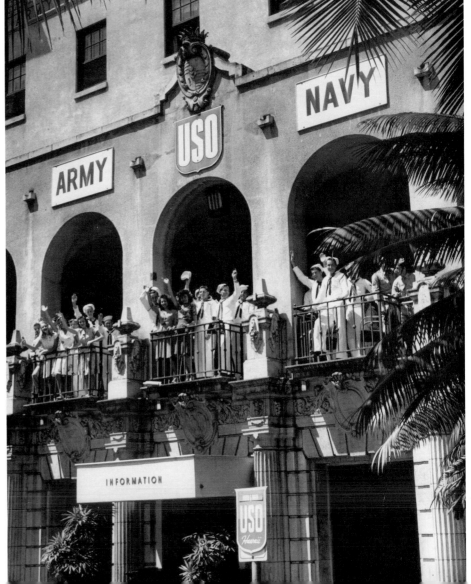

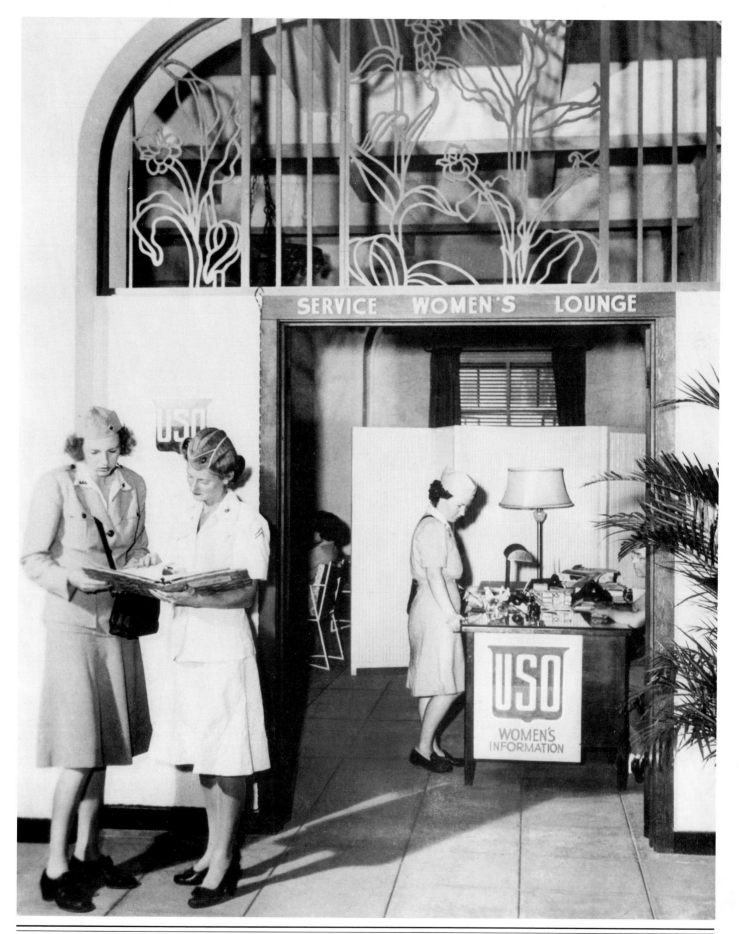

The USO provided for servicemen *and* servicewomen. This is the YWCA's building in Honolulu.

A USO mobile canteen delivering goodies on Oahu.

R&R at its best: sailors on a USO-arranged tour of Maui, Hawaii.

Mrs. Alfred Scott serves punch to a soldier at the Phyllis Wheatley YWCA USO, July 1943.

Happy soldiers — what the USO is all about (Bermuda).

It only *seems* that World War II was fought exclusively on doughnuts and coffee. In San Francisco's USO facility, the Navy clearly wasn't complaining.

Early day care, USO style.

A simple, stunning expression of generosity and gratitude.

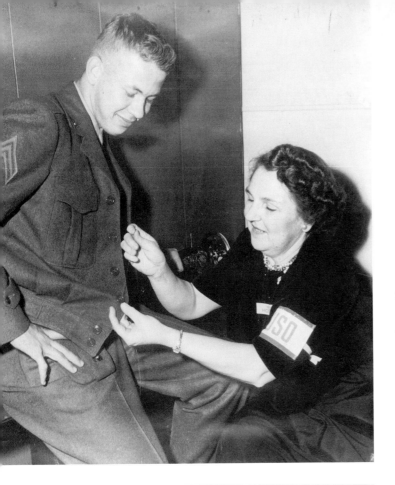

Button sewing—a basic USO service that kept thousands of soldiers ready and willing for inspection.

Illustrator Cardwell Higgins's memorable poster of a USO lady and two servicemen.

The models who posed for Higgins.

Norman Rockwell's memorable USO tribute ran on the cover of *The Saturday Evening Post*'s February 7, 1942, issue.

Despite the terrible effects of Japanese bombing, the Intramuros USO Club in Manila remained open.

Chapter 3

Soldiers in Greasepaint: Entertaining the Troops

The USO had planned to provide live entertainment for the troops, both as a morale boost for the men and as a way of taking the burden off the small towns near the bases, which at best, usually had only a small movie theater. But what started out as a way to bring shows to soldiers had, by the war's end, become the single greatest entertainment enterprise in show business history.

Soon after the USO was officially launched in early 1941, professionals in the entertainment industry — including movie studio executives, producers, and agents — became concerned over how the new organization would fare in hiring talent, producing shows, and handling the other complex details that such vast undertakings would entail.

Walter Hoving, the USO's first president, sought the advice of entertainment industry leaders. Upon their recommendation, the USO created Camp Shows, Inc., on October 30, 1941. This organization was funded through the USO; however, it was governed by a separate board of directors drawn from the ranks of entertainment industry giants intimately familiar with all the intricate tasks peculiar to show business.

The president of Camp Shows, Inc., was Abe Lastfogel, king of the talent agents and chairman of the board at the William Morris Agency. Through his efforts, all the major entertainment

unions — including the Screen Actors Guild, Actors Equity, and the major musicians' unions — agreed to allow entertainers to waive pay and working conditions requirements in order to bring live shows to armed forces personnel.

A parallel effort was being organized by Thomas J. Watson, Sr., president of International Business Machines (IBM) during World War II. In the fall of 1940 he led the way in forming the group Friends of New York Sailors and Soldiers, which became the Citizens Committee for the Army and Navy in January 1941. The committee distributed records and books to men from across the States. By May of 1941 the Citizens Committee was presenting shows in seven trucks loaned by General Motors to serve as mobile stages in Army camps east of the Rockies. One of the first shows was at Fort Dix, New Jersey. The earliest overseas tour began on October 30, 1941, and continued for two weeks at defense installations in the Caribbean with Laurel and Hardy, John Garfield, Ray Bolger, Chico Marx, and Mitzi Mayfair. In November 1941, the group was officially included in USO Camp Shows, Inc. When the United States officially entered the war, plans were immediately made to bring regular live shows to Americans fighting overseas.

Under Lastfogel's direction, four main entertainment circuits were designated for show tours. The Victory Circuit brought such fully staged Broadway shows as *Mexican Hayride, Panama Hattie, Blithe Spirit, The Little Indians,* and *Over 21* to 640 stateside military bases with facilities for large audiences. The Blue Circuit brought smaller companies of vaudeville entertainers to military bases without facilities for large audiences. The Hospital Circuit brought special entertainment units to military personnel in hospitals. The most well-known of all USO-sponsored entertainment efforts were the Camp Shows' units that toured the Foxhole Circuit, boosting the spirits of American soldiers, airmen, and sailors around the world with shows in Alaska, Australia, Baffin Island, Belgium, Bermuda, Brazil, Burma, Canada, the Caribbean, Central Africa, China, Egypt, England, France, Germany, Greenland, Guam, Hawaii, Iceland, Iran, Iraq, Italy, Labrador, Luxembourg, Malta, the Netherlands, New Caledonia, the South Pacific, and the Soviet Union.

Camp Shows, Inc., engaged over seven thousand performers, who became known as "Soldiers in Greasepaint." Many well-known figures of stage, screen, and radio donated their talent, comprising a veritable Who's Who of stars of the 1940s. Bing Crosby, Bob Hope, Ann Sheridan, the Andrews Sisters, James Cagney, Gary Cooper, Fred Astaire, Jimmy Stewart, Humphrey Bogart, Dinah Shore, Paulette Goddard, Ed Gardner of "Duffy's Tavern," Al Jolson, Clark Gable, Carol Lombard, Gertrude Lawrence, and Walt Disney were among the cavalcade of stars who so willingly gave of themselves to bring delight and laughter to American servicemen in every far-flung corner of World War II. Before the war was over, Martha Raye had entertained soldiers in every theater of war where American troops were stationed.

Big-mouthed comedian Joe E. Brown, who was to lose his son in the war, was the first Hollywood star to tour front-line bases, playing for the troops in Alaska and the Aleutians in 1942. Brown had a signature joke, a corny joke really, which made it all the more endearing. Louis Sobol, in *The American Legion Magazine,* described the scene.

[Brown] would point to a GI in the audience and demand: "You over there! Where do you come from?" The answer might be Brooklyn or Pittsburgh or Dallas—it didn't matter. Then Brown would shout: "You mean you admit it?"

Brown later went on to be the first USO per-

former to tour the China-Burma-India theater of operations.

Marlene Dietrich, whose sister was a prisoner at the Belsen concentration camp, took a particular risk in playing to soldiers: Adolf Hitler had placed her on his infamous death list. Nonetheless, Dietrich performed at Utah Beach, Normandy, in July 1944, a mere twenty-eight days after D Day. A few months later, during the Battle of the Bulge, Dietrich and her unit were about to be captured by German troops when they were rescued by soldiers from the U.S. 82d Airborne Division.

Lesser-known entertainers, of course, provided most of the performances. Throughout the war, they brought, incredibly, 428,521 live shows to stateside and overseas audiences of armed forces men and women numbering 212,974,401. Among them, for example, was Maebelle K. Smith, who brought her "Ziegfield in Miniature" shows to service personnel at training bases throughout south Florida.

Another was Billy McIntyre. A soldier-musician who was attached to a USO unit, he played with the "Dogtaggers," the first American band to play jazz in the Soviet Union, at Poltava Air Base, in January 1945.

Many of these "Soldiers in Greasepaint" faced the same dangers as the fighting men they were sent to entertain. Thirty-seven of them died in the course of the war, including musical theater star Tamara Dreisen, who was killed along with twenty other performers in a plane crash in Lisbon, Portugal, in February 1943. Severely injured in the same crash was singer Jane Froman, who later recovered and resumed touring for the USO. Benny Goodman and Sammy Kaye were among the top names in popular music who regularly braved the dangers of combat zones to bring their batons and orchestras to the front to entertain the troops. And, of course, the legendary Glenn Miller (Maj. Glenn Miller, director of the Army Air Corps band), was killed on December 16, 1944, when his plane went down en route from England to France.

All entertainers in overseas units had to follow strict guidelines of conduct to maintain military security. In order to protect the secrecy of troop locations, USO entertainers on the Foxhole Circuit were strictly forbidden from revealing their schedule or itinerary to anyone and afterward could not relate where they had been or to what units they had played. (Nearly fifty years later American performers such as Jay Leno and Steve Martin encountered the same kind of restrictions when they visited American troops stationed in Saudi Arabia during Operation Desert Shield.)

In addition, since civilians attached to military units overseas were liable to be mistaken for spies if captured by the enemy, USO performers were required to wear special uniforms identifying them as noncombatants. A case in point is what happened to the comedy duo of Jane and Joe McKenna, who at Normandy in late July 1944, less than two months after D Day, went out for a ride after dark and were captured by a German patrol. The McKennas later recalled that, although the Germans spoke no English and they no German, they communicated to their captors in pantomime and other gestures that they were entertainers and not soldiers; the drawn guns were lowered. Twelve days later, Jane and Joe McKenna were liberated by the advancing Allies.

Foxhole Circuit entertainers played to all sizes of audiences, from as many as fifteen thousand GIs at a large stadium or airfield to as few as fifteen or twenty soldiers standing around a jeep at a remote battlefield crossroads.

Field-hospital performances were the scene of many poignant memories for USO performers. Ventriloquist Edgar Bergen, with the help of his wooden-headed partner Charlie McCarthy, managed to get a smile and a laugh out of a soldier who, after experiencing a particularly fierce bombing raid, had not eaten or spoken for over a week. It was actually "McCarthy" who made the breakthrough when he said to Bergen, "Oh, nuts, boss, say something bright. Our pal here is bored." The soldier struggled to a sitting position, grinned weakly, and said, "Hi." It was the first word he had uttered in eight days. Bergen would later refer to the incident as one of the highlights of his long and distinguished career.

Unfortunately, not all of the memories were happy. A young woman singer with the USO, on a visit to an Army hospital in Italy, was asked by a wounded soldier to sing "Abide with Me." When she began to sing, he abruptly stopped her, and said he did not want her to perform it then but later, at his funeral. Hiding her shock, she tried to joke him out of his morbid prediction, to no avail. A few days later, the soldier, barely into manhood, died; the equally young singer granted his wish.

The Camp Shows' units brought to millions of young servicemen on the front lines of World War II both a slice of American life and a lot of hope—Bob Hope, that is.

On May 6, 1941, five months before the USO took its official plunge into show business, Hope's radio show, sponsored by Pepsodent Toothpaste, was broadcast in front of a live audience of Army personnel at March Field, in Riverside, California. His brand of humor—which novelist John Steinbeck described as "topical, both broad and caustic, but never aimed at people, but at conditions and ideas"—articulated for the men what they were experiencing in those days when war clouds loomed in the immediate future. He later remarked that the servicemen and women he played to appreciated his act mainly because it communicated to Americans at home what they were going through, and he characterized himself as the Army's "ski-nosed Western Union." Soon afterward, Hope played to troops at Camp Pendleton and San Diego Naval Base—which Hope later called "one of the largest pools of lonesome men in the United States"—where the broadcast was again a laugh-packed success. For the rest of the war, Hope's Pepsodent Show regularly appeared at military bases throughout the country.

The first of Hope's wartime USO tours was in 1942, when he traveled to Alaska and the Aleutians—what Hope dubbed the "Great White Way." Along with sidekick Jerry Colonna, singer Frances Langford, and musician Tony Romano, he put on his show for American troops guarding the North Pacific at Anchorage, Annette, Cold Bay, Cordova, Naknek, Nome, Unimak, and White Horse. Hope and his troupe made their first combat-zone tour in 1943, when they brought their show to U.S. forces in North Africa. After the show, they followed Gen. George Patton's Seventh Army into Sicily. Somewhere along the line, probably in Italy, Hope started using one of his signature jokes: "You remember World War II," he'd say to the dirty, tired troops. "It was in all the papers." While in Palermo, Hope was one of the first comedians to have *firsthand* experience of what it was like to really bomb, or more precisely, be bombed, when the Germans staged an air raid on a target right next to his hotel. Immediately afterward, Patton had Hope and his company sent back to Algiers for their own safety.

Hope next went to the South Pacific, where on Wendy Island, his show was seen by a young naval officer and future president of the United States, John F. Kennedy, and his PT-boat crew. At the war's end in 1945, Hope was playing to American GIs in Germany and noted the change of mood and outlook of his audiences. Back in the early dark days of the war, the men had been anxious about the impending challenges that lay ahead. With the war won, they were more relaxed, expressing an attitude that seemed to say, "We'll see you again." And they sure did. Over the next four decades, Hope continued to contribute his unique humor and cheer with shows for American service personnel in all parts of the world.

In 1946, Supreme Allied Commander Dwight D. Eisenhower presented Hope with the Medal of Merit, the first of many high honors Hope would receive over the years in recognition of his efforts to keep up the spirit of America's armed forces personnel.

Steinbeck, writing in the *New York Herald Tribune* in 1943, captured best the essence of what Bob Hope meant to the troops:

> The story is told in one of those nameless hospitals . . . Hope and company had worked until gradually they had got leaden eyes to sparkling, had planted and nurtured and coaxed laughter to life.
>
> A gunner, who had a stomach wound, was gasping softly with laughter. A railroad casualty slapped the cast of his left hand with his right hand by way of applause. And once the laughter was alive, the men laughed even before the punch line, and it had to be repeated so they could laugh again.

Finally, it came time for Frances Langford to sing. The men asked for "As Time Goes By." She stood up beside the little GI piano and started to sing. Her voice was a little hoarse and strained. She had been working too hard and too long.

She got through eight bars when a boy with a head wound began to cry. She stopped, and then went on. But her voice wouldn't work anymore. She finished the song whispering. Then she walked out, so no one could see her, and broke down. The ward was quiet. No one applauded.

Then Hope walked into the aisle between the beds and he said seriously: "Fellows, the folks at home are having a terrible time about eggs. They can't get any powdered eggs at all. They've got to use the old-fashioned kind you break open."

The hospital exploded into laughter. "There's a man for you," Steinbeck concluded, "there is *really* a man."

Coffee with Olivia DeHavilland. Is everybody happy?

Jimmy Stewart demonstrating dunking technique; the ladies seem eager to learn.

One of the most famous USO photos: in the sweltering heat of Burma, Ann Sheridan hugs a deliriously grateful GI.

Hope busses a beauty, again. A Hollywood USO fund-raiser provided the comedian with an air-tight alibi.

USO high-steppers with two game recruits in Australia, 1943.

Dinah Shore entertains the troops in France, August 1944.

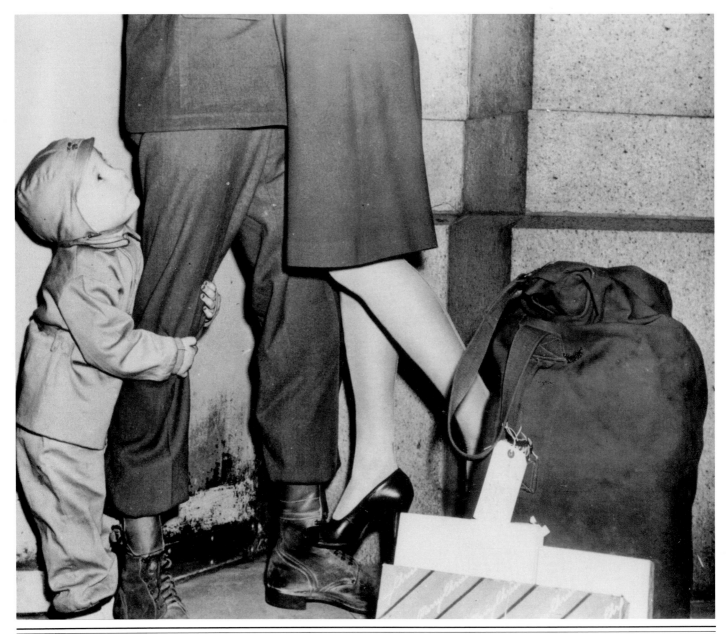

A family is reunited at Christmas 1944.

The bus to Ipanema — a USO tour leaves on a thirty-day tour of Brazilian bases and USO clubs.

USO services in Bermuda.

Marlene Dietrich in France with U.S. servicewomen, 1944.

Hope in Hawaii. In 1944 he had not yet become a national idol and was introduced as "the radio entertainer."

"Der Bingle" — Bing Crosby on the European "cow pasture" circuit in 1944.

Dietrich "roughing it" with the troops in 1945.

The Andrews Sisters (Maxene, second from left; Patty, second from right) recreated the USO "victory canteens" in the Broadway hit *Over Here.*

USO Camp Shows drew standing-room-only crowds all over the world.

Maebelle Smith, unsung hero.

In San Juan, Puerto Rico, the USO "commandeered" a spectacular casino.

"And it shall be built." A USO club goes up in Luzon, the Philppines.

A soldier records a message for home courtesy of the USO's "Star Spangled Network."

Walter Cronkite (right) traveled with and reported on the "USO."

PFC Mickey Rooney breaks up an audience of infantrymen from the 44th Division in Kist, Germany, on April 13, 1945. V-E Day is less than four weeks away.

The American and Russian armies finally met at the Elbe River near Torgau, Germany, on April 25, 1945. The happy soldiers are 2d Lt. William Robertson (left) and Lt. Alexander Sylvashko.

A jaunty Bob Hope displaying his world class grin.

Times Square, New York, September 2, 1945 — V-J Day. The nightmare is over!

"Those who forget the past are condemned to repeat it." A bugler blows taps at Margraten Cemetery, Holland.

Chapter 4

The USO at the End of the War

By V-E Day, in May 1945, the USO was producing as many as seven hundred shows each day for American service personnel stationed around the world. Far from winding down its operations as peace in Europe was secured, the USO found itself serving more and more service personnel with increasing amounts of off-duty time.

The job of winning the war against Japan still lay ahead in mid-1945, and hundreds of thousands of American soldiers were shipped on transports through the Panama Canal on their way to the Pacific. Although the troops were not permitted ashore while they made the passage between the oceans, the USO was there with pier-side shows on both sides of the canal, playing to these floating GI audiences.

Stateside demand for USO services exploded with demobilization as great numbers of military personnel in transit crowded onto public rail and bus lines on the last leg of the long trip home. In the first two years after the war, as the USO began to limit its operations, attention was turned to helping enlisted men and their families make the transition back to civilian life.

On January 9, 1948, the first wartime USO came to an end with this announcement by the organization's president, Dr. Lindsey F. Kimball: "Operation USO has discharged its mission, fulfilled its original purpose, and ended its task."

Although the USO may not have taken any beachheads, or won any battles, its efforts to maintain the morale of America's armed forces nonetheless played a vital role in the ultimate Allied victory. As Secretary of War Henry Lewis Stimson put it: "No arguments will be sufficient unless backed by the invincible spirit of the human soul."

For both the "Soldiers in Greasepaint" and the thousands of volunteers at clubs and hospitals, what really made the USO work was the spirit in which the services were offered.

In World War II, the USO strengthened that spirit and reinforced the will to win. For both those whom it served and those who gave of themselves to make it work, the United Service Organizations was an integral part of the nation's war effort, an army of volunteers dedicated to the most basic common good: freedom from tyranny.

The Copacabana All Girl Review always drew a crowd. On August 29, 1945, the venue was the Glenn Miller Theater near Marseilles, France.

Gen. Douglas MacArthur signed the Japanese formal surrender documents on the USS *Missouri* in Tokyo Bay on September 2, 1945. That day MacArthur, in a broadcast to the American people, said: "Today the guns are silent. A great tragedy has ended. A great victory has been won. . . . "

A USO Navy tour begins from Recife, Brazil.

A USO mobile unit in the Canal Zone, Panama.

The immortal Danny Kaye performing for the marines in Sasebo, Japan, on October 25, 1945. The chalked message across the front of the stage reads: "Officers Keep Out. Enlisted Men's Country."

Kaye and Leo Durocher, the Dodger's manager, visit a Brooklyn resident and baseball fan, J. Arbenny. Despite the sign — sent by then–New York mayor Fiorello LaGuardia — it's a long hike to Ebbets Field from Atsugi Airfield, Japan.

USO

This Citation for Distinguished Service
is awarded to

Harvey S. Firestone, Jr.

in grateful recognition of support given to
those serving in the armed forces and to hospitalized veterans
through the United Service Organizations

1946-47

L. F. Kimball
PRESIDENT

Care Whitman
NATIONAL CAMPAIGN CHAIRMAN

☆ ☆ ☆ ☆ ☆ ☆ ☆ ☆ ☆ ☆ ☆ ☆ ☆ ☆ ☆

A USO Distinguished Service Citation presented to Harvey Firestone for his efforts during 1946–47.

Chapter 5

The Rebirth of the USO: Korea and the Cold War

All USO facilities, both in the United States and overseas, had ceased operating by the end of 1947. On December 31, 1947, President Harry S Truman wrote Lindsey F. Kimball, president of the USO, informing him that

the USO has now fulfilled its commitment and discharged its wartime responsibility completely and with signal distinction. It therefore becomes my privilege to award an honorable discharge to the organization, to its member agencies, to the Camp Shows affiliate, to the million and a half volunteers, and to the thousands of devoted staff members. . . .

Having been honorably discharged by the president of the United States, the USO was pared down to a skeleton staff to pay out final financial obligations and to liquidate its assets. The close of World War II did not, however, bring an end to the need for what the USO provided. In the years 1948 to 1950, 1.6 million Americans remained in uniform, nearly five times as many as in the days just prior to the U.S. entry into World War II.

The onset of the cold war, marked by the Berlin blockade in 1948 and rising tension in the Far East, made the maintenance of a large peacetime army necessary. The tense Berlin situation produced what would become one of the most celebrated annual entertainment spectacles in U.S. history—Bob Hope's Christmas Show.

During the six-month period after Truman wrote to Kimball, Secretary of Defense James Forrestal had requested and received the results of a study by the Civilian Advisory Committee. The committee's charge was to review the armed forces' morale, welfare, and recreation efforts in World War II, to propose a plan for similar efforts in the event of a national emergency, and to recommend how to serve the needs of a greatly expanded peacetime military. The committee recommended either reactivating the USO on a broader, programmatic scale or instituting another civilian authority responsible to the president of the United States for the same purpose.

In June 1948, Kimball gathered the representatives of the USO's six founding agencies at a meeting to discuss Forrestal's request that the USO be reactivated in response to the committee's recommendations. By December, the USO's board of directors had agreed on the framework for a peacetime USO, and on January 1, 1949, the USO was officially back in business. In April 1949, the newly elected board chose Harvey S. Firestone, Jr., chairman of the Firestone Tire and Rubber Co., as its new president.

On May 19, 1949, Firestone paid a personal visit to President Truman. Firestone reported that the

USO had been reorganized and reactivated and was ready to assume leadership on behalf of the American people in cooperation with established national agencies. He expressed his confidence "that the American people, either through their Community Chests or through separate campaigns, will meet this responsibility to the young men and women in the armed forces and to veterans in hospitals."

Bridging the gap between the military and civilian community would prove to be a tremendous task. In its attempt to meet all the requests made by the government and the military, the USO needed to expand rapidly. Its expenditures began to exceed income despite drastic reductions in operations and overhead. USO fund-raisers cited apathy at the grass roots as well as among business leaders as the reason for the great difficulty in raising funds for the organization. Other factors also contributed: the USO program in the late 1940s had much less visibility than in wartime and almost none in the large cities where Community Chest strength was concentrated; it also was overly dependent on Community Chests for support, but many did not include the USO in their quotas. On January 31, 1950, despite auspicious beginnings, the "new USO," after barely a year as a peacetime organization, was forced to suspend operations. The USO Executive Committee recommended that the USO "retain its corporate entity so as to be available for service if called upon in the event of a national emergency."

And then, in June 1950, communist aggression erupted in the Far East when North Korea invaded South Korea. Along with other member-states of the United Nations, the United States was soon drawn into the conflict. Rapid remobilization brought several hundred thousand more men into the military, which peaked at 3.5 million armed forces personnel by the end of the Korean conflict in 1953. Both Secretary of Defense Gen. George C. Marshall and Secretary of the Navy Adm. Francis P. Matthews realized the urgent need to reinstitute civilian-based social programs for the armed forces. They called upon the USO and the former USO affiliate, Camp Shows, Inc., to join forces again to provide much-needed social and recreational support for America's servicemen and women.

A "Memorandum of Understanding" was entered into between the new USO and the Department of Defense. Under its terms, the USO became solely responsible to the president of the United States and the secretary of defense. Camp Shows, Inc., be-

came the official liaison agency for procuring talent from the entertainment industry for all shows for the military, both stateside and overseas.

With the endorsement of the federal government, the new USO received increased funding through the United Fund and Community Chests. Nonetheless, it was still forced to scale down its activities. From 1951 to 1953 there were as many armed forces personnel as there had been in 1942, yet the new USO had to operate on a budget of $13.6 million; this was less than half the budget of its predecessor when the United States entered World War II at the end of 1941.

The enlisted men called up to serve in the Korean War tended to be much younger than those who had taken part in World War II; 60 percent were under twenty-one, 80 percent were under twenty-five. In addition, many of the older soldiers were reservists, who, having already served in World War II, had to leave their jobs and young families behind when recalled to active duty.

At the onset of the Korean War, the USO—with far less funding and less direct governmental support than it had had in World War II—was faced with the challenge of providing off-duty young men and women of the armed forces with the best spiritual and moral influences of civilian life in an atmosphere devoid of military discipline. Such contacts were vital not only to maintain the service personnel's links with home, but also to preserve the moral character of recruits during their military service and thereby preserve the democratic values essential to the well-being of the nation.

The USO consolidated its big-city operations, where recreational opportunities for off-duty soldiers were already available, and channeled more of its resources into smaller communities near large military installations. In addition, the services of local community groups and church and fraternal organizations were enlisted to complement the USO's efforts. Local clergy near military bases were called upon to work with military chaplains in support of the USO's social and religious programs.

Unlike the USO in World War II, which had concentrated most of its social support services stateside, the USO of the early 1950s extended itself to over one million servicemen and women who found themselves manning the ramparts of the free world in Korea and other far-flung garrisons in foreign lands. USO centers were established for the first time outside of the United States—in France, Italy, North Africa, and the Philippines. Extensive USO operations were also opened in Japan to meet the off-duty needs of U.S. troops serving in Korea.

The New York Times.

"All the News That's Fit to Print"

LATE CITY EDITION
Sunny with pleasant temperatures today. Fair tomorrow.
Temperature Range Today—Max.,80; Min.,60
Temperature Yesterday—Max.,90.3; Min.,69
Full U. S. Weather Bureau Report, Page 35

Copyright, 1950, by The New York Times Company.

VOL. XCIX. No. 33,758.

Entered as Second-Class Matter,
Post Office, New York, N. Y.

NEW YORK, WEDNESDAY, JUNE 28, 1950.

Times Square, New York 18, N. Y.
Telephone Lackawanna 4-1000

FIVE CENTS

TRUMAN ORDERS U. S. AIR, NAVY UNITS TO FIGHT IN AID OF KOREA; U. N. COUNCIL SUPPORTS HIM; OUR FLIERS IN ACTION; FLEET GUARDS FORMOSA

114 RESCUED HERE AS LINER GROUNDS AFTER COLLISION

Excalibur, With Hole 15 Feet

SANCTIONS VOTED

Council Adopts Plan of U. S. for Armed Force in Korea, 7 to 1

President Takes Chief Role In Determining U. S. Course

Truman's Leadership for Forceful Policy to Meet Threat to World Peace Draws Together Advisers on Vital Move

U.S. FORCE FIGHTING

MacArthur Installs an Advanced Echelon in Southern Korea

Statement on Korea

By The Associated Press.

WASHINGTON, June 27—The text of President Truman's statement today on Korea:

In Korea the Government forces, which were armed to prevent border raids and to preserve internal security, were attacked by invading forces from North Korea. The Security Council of the United Nations called upon the invading troops to cease hostilities and to withdraw to the Thirty-eighth

BID MADE TO RUSSIA

President Asks Moscow to Act to Terminate Fighting in Korea

June 28, 1950, saw the beginning of U.S. involvement in Korea.

Camp Shows, Inc., now an integral member organization within the USO, sent out 126 entertainment units, which put on over fifty-four hundred shows for the service personnel in Korea. In 1953 not a single day passed without a Camp Shows' unit staging a show somewhere in Korea, bringing much laughter and a longed-for renewal of ties with home.

USO entertainers shared the rigors of the Korean winter with the servicemen and women to whom they played, using heated ambulances as dressing rooms and performing on impromptu stages in freezing weather in bivouac areas. Their contributions in the Korean War were invaluable, as Col. Charles W. Christenberry, the U.S. Army's chief of special services, stated at a USO board of directors' meeting in 1951: "There is no substitute for live professional entertainment as a morale builder. . . . It brings something to the men in uniform that even movies can't equal."

This sentiment was echoed by Pvt. Robert W. Copeland, who wrote to his family in Silver Spring, Maryland, soon after the truce in 1953: "They really do a great job. I never realized how much hearing American songs sung by young men and good-looking young girls would mean."

As in World War II, top names from the entertainment world traveled to the front lines in Korea to bolster the spirit of America's fighting men. One of the first was actress Jennifer Jones, who visited hospitalized servicemen in Korea as well as in Japan. Headliners in Korea included Jack Benny, Errol Flynn, Danny Kaye, Robert Merrill, and the legendary Al Jolson, who had been one of the most active entertainers during World War II. Tragically, Jolson's last trip to Korea proved too taxing for his weakening heart. His doctors, and even his accompanist Harry Akst, had warned him not to make the trip. Jolson went anyway. And in a matter of weeks after his return, he was dead. On his deathbed Jolson kidded that he had spent more time with Gen. Douglas MacArthur than President Truman had during his visit. Then, murmuring, "I'm going, I'm going," Jolson breathed his last.

In late 1951 the first of the USO's Christmas shows toured U.S. military installations not only in Korea and the Far East, but also in Alaska, Europe, and North Africa, with stars such as Paul Douglas, Ray Milland, Molly Picon, Walter Pidgeon, Jan Sterling, and Keenan Wynn. In all, Celebrity Units drawn from the USO Hollywood Coordinating Committee brought 866 performances to service personnel in Korea, featuring such stars as Rory Calhoun, Piper Laurie, Debbie Reynolds, Mickey Rooney, and Frances Langford, who a decade earlier had sung at the edge of World War II battlefields with Bob Hope.

The truce, which ended the hostilities in Korea in 1953, by no means ended the need for the USO. In the years that followed, cold war tensions kept millions of Americans in the armed forces at bases all over the world and the United States. At the beginning of 1954, 3.5 million Americans were in the armed forces, with one in eleven American families having a son in the military. More and more military personnel were stationed in smaller, isolated units in remote parts of the United States and overseas, and the USO was there, reaching out with touring shows and mobile service units.

In 1954 the USO came to the forefront of the entertainment world with Bob Hope's first televised USO show, broadcast from Thule Air Force Base in northwestern Greenland, in which he introduced the glamorous Anita Ekberg. Years later when asked why he always had beautiful women in his show, Hope quipped: "The pretty girls remind the guys what they're fighting for. I took an apple pie and mom once, and two divisions 'went over the hill.'" Also in the show were Hollywood columnist Hedda Hopper, Hope regular Jerry Colonna, Les Brown and his orchestra, and the U.S. Air Force Band. For the rest of the 1950s, Hope continued to tour the Northeast Air Command with yearly shows in Labrador and Newfoundland as well as Alaska. In 1957 his show played at bases in the Far East with Jayne Mansfield as a featured attraction.

Lesser-known groups of entertainers were also called upon to bring their talents to American servicemen and women overseas in the years after 1953. Among them were groups of college students who brought fully staged performances of popular stage plays to overseas military personnel. At bases in Europe, student performers from the Catholic University of America presented *The Taming of the Shrew*, a troupe from Denison University performed *The Man Who Came to Dinner*, and student actors and actresses from Yale toured with *Out of the Frying Pan*. At installations in the Pacific Command, a theater company from the University of Minnesota performed *I Remember Mama*.

Stateside, the USO was there with mobile units and traveling shows at military maneuvers, including Operation Snowfall, a winter training exercise held near upstate New York's Camp Drum in 1952, and at the Army and Air Force's Exercise Longhorn in Texas. Sailors and marines on naval exercises in the Caribbean were also treated to USO shows.

In June 1955, the Belles of Indiana—a women's chorale group from the University of Indiana at Bloomington—toured overseas bases in Japan and Korea for the USO. They brought a welcome taste of home to American servicemen and women with such standards as "That Old Black Magic," "St. Louis Blues," and of course, "Back Home in Indiana." They put on seventy-five shows in seventy-seven days, performing from the backs of trucks near abandoned enemy minefields, in large arenas, as well as in the palace of the president of South Korea.

Throughout the 1950s, USO veteran of World War II Maebelle K. Smith, with her Mask and Wig Club, again produced entertainment for Air Force and Navy personnel at bases all over Florida. They delighted their audiences with such shows as *Artists and Models, Garden of Girls,* and *Caribbean Capers.*

By the end of the 1950s, the USO had established itself as a permanent organization dedicated to meeting the social and recreational needs of service personnel wherever they might be. For example, in 1958, when U.S. Marines were suddenly sent to Lebanon, a USO troupe was quickly diverted from its tour to Germany to perform at the operation's staging area at Adana, Turkey. Ironically, twenty-five years later, Loretta Lynn's USO tour to Germany would also be diverted to perform for marines deployed in Lebanon.

At the end of the Korean War, there were 113,394 USO volunteers in the United States, and 294 USO centers operating both stateside and overseas. Having started as a wartime emergency agency in the dark days of World War II, the USO had reemerged as an integral part of the nation's social structure. The general purpose of the USO had changed as well, as stated by its executive director Edwin E. Bond in 1954:

> The parents of the nation's young men and women, who are away from home for the first time in their lives, can find new assurance in the knowledge that they will have friends wherever they go, because the USO goes with them.

The rugged Korean terrain. Men of the 19th Infantry Regiment work their way up another tortuous mountain.

"How I love ya." Al Jolson, weeks before his death, performing for U.S. troops at Pusan Stadium, 1950. Jolson made the Korean trip at his own expense.

Hope is performing; the audience is enjoying in Seoul, Korea, October 1950.

Just one of the boys. Hope in Korea, October 1950.

"This hallowed ground." At the United Nations cemetery in Pusan, Korea, a little girl places flowers on the grave of an American soldier, April 1951.

A real MASH (Mobile Army Surgical Hospital) unit in Wonju, Korea, September 1951.

Surgery twenty miles from the front line. The 8209th MASH in action, August 1952.

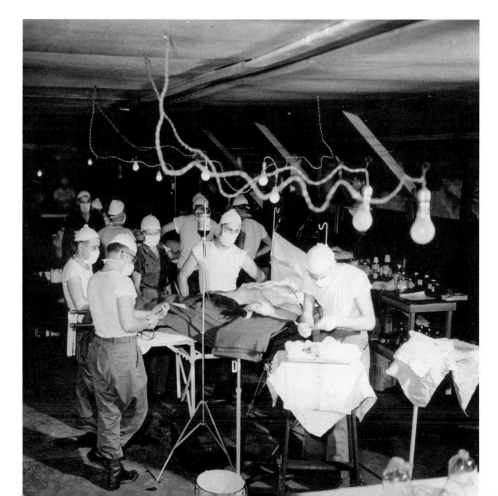

Tokyo General Hospital. Marine PFC Howard Wells is the host; Bob Hope and Marilyn Maxwell, the visitors. Wells, with the 2d Battalion, 1st Marine Division, was wounded in Korea.

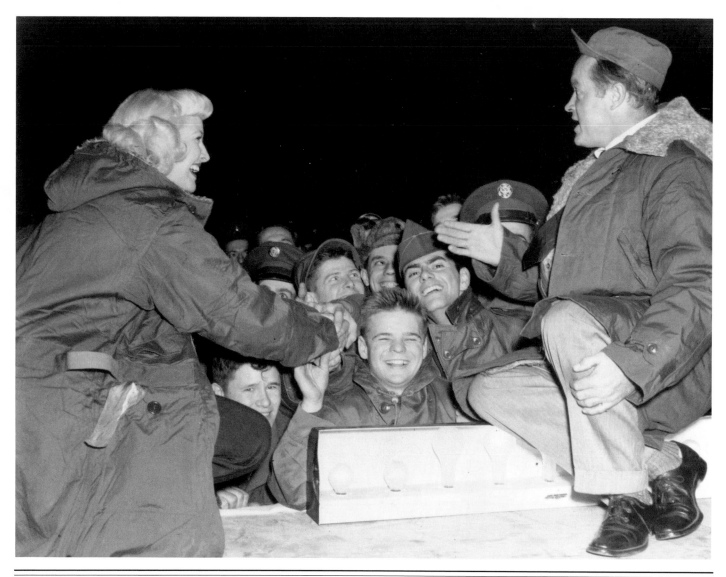

Gentlemen prefer blondes. Troops greet M. Maxwell, ignore B. Hope.

Groucho Marx—without mustache—and his wife visit a patient in San Francisco's VA Hospital. Despite an ultimate total of 54,246 American dead, Korea was officially a "police action"; special legislation had to be passed in 1951 to open veterans hospitals to those wounded in Korea.

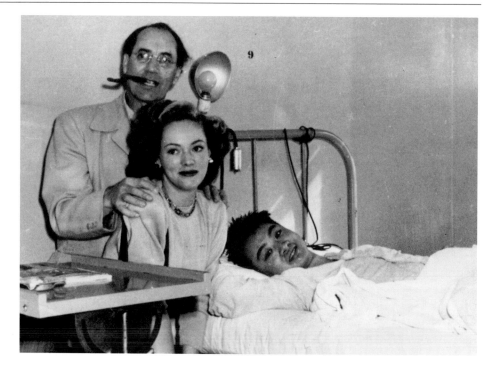

An impromptu chapel provides a moment's peace.

Rain or shine, the USO show goes on.

Actor Paul Douglas delivers a warm message in the cold. Douglas and wife, actress Jan Sterling, toured Korea in 1952.

The "Buffalo Bowl" was one Korean stop during disc-jockey Johnny Grant's Operation Starlift for the USO.

Near the front. A solitary dancer . . . with a cast of thousands.

The Rebirth of the USO: Korea and the Cold War **65**

Marilyn Monroe's USO tour was titled "Anything Goes." The troops could only hope.

"Where do I sign?" "Anywhere!" Marilyn Monroe provides her autograph, Korea, 1954.

Danny Kaye — the one out of uniform — and GI musicians.

Jerry Colonna, Dorothy Provine, Anita Bryant, Jayne Mansfield, and Bob Hope head north to Alaska.

The luminescent Jayne Mansfield with lucky escort Maj. Gen. Herbert Jones in December 1957.

In the field . . . again. USO Camp Shows.

Jack Benny and friends in Korea.

Mickey Rooney was supposed to be feeding the troops, not Dick Winslow.

"Oh, my aching back!" Errol Flynn entertains wounded troops in Korea with a story of wrenched vertebrae, his own.

Chapter 6

The USO After Korea

If the United States was at peace in the years after the Korean War truce in 1953, one could not tell from the size of the nation's armed forces. The ranks of the military remained at wartime strength, with more than one million service personnel stationed overseas.

In 1961 President John F. Kennedy, the USO's honorary chairman, wrote in support of the organization: "Winning the peace is a lonely battle."

In August of that year, cold war tensions had intensified with the construction of the Berlin Wall. When the Cuban missile crisis threatened to turn the cold war "hot" in October 1962, USO mobile units and professional staff were called into action to meet the off-duty needs of the military personnel suddenly deployed to staging areas in the southeastern United States, especially in Florida. Again in 1965, when U.S. forces were called upon to restore order in the Dominican Republic, the USO sent personnel to provide aid to Americans there who suddenly found themselves as refugees.

After 1957, funding for the USO from the United Fund and Community Chests steadily decreased, and in 1962, the organization was faced with the prospect of actually going out of business for lack of financial support. That year, a survey was commissioned to determine whether there was a need for a voluntary civilian program to serve military personnel in peacetime as in war. Under the direction of Michigan State University president Dr.

John A. Hannah, a panel of experts on social welfare programs unanimously agreed that the USO was needed "not merely during wartime, but perhaps even more certainly during the cold war or 'normal peacetime,' both in the continental United States and overseas." They also recommended revamping the structure of the USO to meet the global needs of a large peacetime military force.

As suggested by the Hannah Survey, the USO made many local USO branches in larger towns and cities autonomous and responsible for their own fund-raising. The national USO continued to administer overseas USO clubs and centers where the needs for service personnel were greatest: in Greece, Guam, Italy, Japan, Korea, Okinawa, the Panama Canal Zone, the Philippines, Puerto Rico, Spain, Turkey, and the Virgin Islands.

Camp Shows, Inc., as part of the national organization, continued as the sole agency through which overseas shows were organized and produced. On the entertainment front, the USO continued to send Bob Hope and his troupe to distant military installations. In 1960 Hope, along with Andy Williams, Janis Paige, and Zsa Zsa Gabor, appeared before audiences of GIs stationed in the Caribbean region, staging shows in Antigua, Panama, Puerto Rico, and at Guantánamo Bay in Cuba. The following year, Hope took his show back to the Northeast Air Command, with appearances at Argentia, Newfoundland; Goose Bay, Labrador; and a return engagement at Thule, Greenland.

A fund-raiser for the New York USO. The Big Apple responds.

A sign behind the desk of the New York USO offers enlisted men a room in Gotham for a single dollar — another USO miracle.

"C'est magnifique." Lucky sailors sightseeing on the French Riviera.

"Hi, Mom." Courtesy of the USO, a soldier calls home from Naples, Italy.

The fourteenth anniversary of the USO as celebrated in Geneva, New York, not far from Sampson Air Force Base.

Hope presents Ginger Rogers to the troops at Eielson Air Force Base, Alaska, Christmas 1956.

In Anchorage, Alaska, the USO club provided some unique culinary services.

The late, great Mary Martin brought Peter Pan to troops in Alaska during 1958.

President Dwight David Eisenhower, holding a special emblem identifying him as USO honorary chairman, with USO council members Harvey Firestone, Emil Schram, and John L. Sullivan (1956).

The aircraft carrier USS *Lexington*, with the crew spelling out "USO" on the flight deck, makes her way into San Francisco Bay in the summer of 1958.

Another USO star, Lena Horne.

For the USO, the help of the great and the near great was welcome.

A cavalcade of stars appeared with Bob Hope in this USO benefit. Left to right: Louis Armstrong, Zsa Zsa Gabor, Ray Bolger, Leo Durocher, Shirley MacLaine, Jimmy Stewart, Jack Benny, Danny Kaye, Rosalind Russell, Hope, and Jimmy Durante.

Perennial Hope sidekick Jerry Colonna clowning around during the 1959 Christmas Show in Alaska.

Up close and personal, a USO Camp Show grounds the Navy.

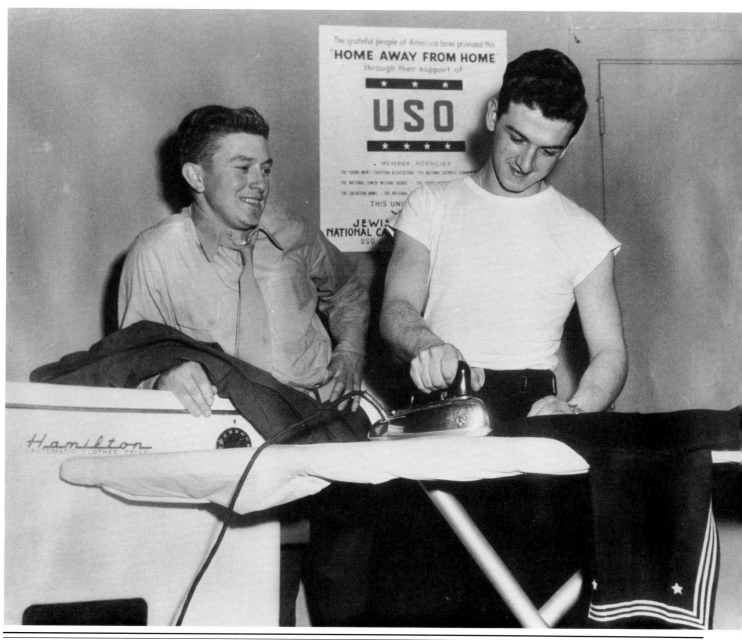

The Great Army-Navy Iron Off. Everybody won.

A USO volunteer ties up a couple of airmen for a good skate.

Chapter 7

The USO in Vietnam: 1963–72

All doubts as to the fundamental need for the USO were eliminated in 1964 with the rapid buildup of troops in Vietnam. The USO had opened its first club in Vietnam in Saigon in September 1963. When the USO announced plans to enlarge its services throughout what was then South Vietnam in 1965, President Lyndon Johnson welcomed the move, stating,

> The decision of the USO leadership to undertake this task will be appreciated by the thousands of servicemen and women who will benefit from the various USO programs. The expanded USO activities are urgently needed, and your decision constitutes a most welcome and worthwhile contribution to our national effort.

Within one year, the USO had opened additional clubs at Da Nang, Nha Trang, and Tan Son Nhut. Other clubs were later established at Di An, Cam Ranh Bay, Qui Nhon, Hill 327 (Da Nang), Vung Tau, and Chu Lai. By the beginning of the U.S. withdrawal in 1972, there were in all eighteen clubs in Vietnam and seven in Thailand.

For the first time in its history, USO facilities operated close to combat areas. GIs coming to the clubs straight from patrol were required to check

their firearms at the door. The clubs themselves were protected by armed military guards. One of the greatest attractions the clubs offered to U.S. military personnel was the chance to enjoy American-style food, especially hamburgers and milkshakes.

The Chu Lai USO, south of Da Nang, served the needs of over sixteen thousand American troops stationed there with the Americal Division. Opened in 1967, it was a beachfront club on the coast of the South China Sea. Personnel visiting the Chu Lai USO were provided with a game room and television area, as well as outdoor recreational facilities maintained by the Army. In addition, tape recorders and tapes were available for GIs to record their personal messages to loved ones back home. The Sand Stage at Chu Lai, located right on the beach, was the site of weekly floor shows seen by thousands of off-duty servicemen and women. Many GIs regularly took advantage of the beach's excellent surfing conditions with surfboards provided by the Chu Lai USO. Among the special programs held at the Chu Lai USO were holiday dinners and parties with special themes, including an Italian Thanksgiving dinner and a Hawaiian Christmas celebration.

In 1964 Bob Hope brought his annual USO Christmas Show to Vietnam for the first time. On Christmas Eve, a bombing attempt was made on Hope and his troupe at their hotel in Saigon. He and his companions were saved when they arrived ten minutes later than expected, soon after a bomb had ripped through a hotel across the street from where they had planned to stay. When informed of the abortive Viet Cong plot, Hope remarked, "It's hard to believe they were critical of my act. . . . The same thing happened to me when I was in vaudeville. The audiences were always trying to get me."

Hope continued to make annual Christmas visits to Vietnam for the next seven years, joined by such celebrities as Joey Heatherton, Jack Jones, Raquel Welch, and Carroll Baker.

Other entertainers who had made USO show tours in World War II also answered the call in Vietnam. Martha Raye made eight tours to Vietnam, serving as a surgical nurse with the Green Berets on her last visit. Twice hit by shrapnel while in Vietnam, Raye later remarked, "[That it was] not so terrible. Just the ribs and a foot. I've had worse hangovers."

Veteran USO World War II trouper Frances Langford toured Vietnam, where she once told an audience of young GIs, "You had better like me. I played for your fathers!"

Another celebrity who visited the troops in Vietnam was actor Raymond Burr, who made a practice of relaying messages given to him by soldiers to their friends and families in the States. Athletes also took part in USO celebrity tours, including boxing great Floyd Patterson and football star Jack Kemp of the Buffalo Bills, who went on to become a U.S. congressman and cabinet member. Other well-known entertainers who volunteered their talents on behalf of the service personnel in Vietnam were Sammy Davis, Jr., Henry Fonda, Ann-Margret, Gary Merrill, Nancy Sinatra, and John Wayne.

In all, from May 1965 to June 1972, 569 USO Shows' units put on over 5,600 performances in Vietnam as well as at military hospitals in Guam, Hawaii, Japan, and Okinawa (the Pacific Hospital Circuit).

Mobile USO units were used in Vietnam to reach soldiers at remote firebases. Maureen ("Mo") Nerli, associate director of the Tan Son Nhut USO from June 1969 to December 1970, later recalled such an experience.

> We were asked, day after day, to go out to a firebase, or a camp. When we did, we would talk to the guys and sing for them, maybe do a show or something, serve food. We usually went out by chopper, but we went by jeep too. One time we

flew up to a little place called Song Mao. The captain arranged for us to fly with an Aussie crew in that strange plane — I think it was called a Caribou — that took off straight up and landed straight down. When we went there I had to bring a rock band — the drums and guitar player and singer, the whole bit. The captain told me, "You can't set foot on this base unless you've got a show." We were asked to do this time after time.

USO clubs in Vietnam not only provided service personnel with temporary respite from a war that was always close at hand, but also helped them maintain ties with home through special programs. In one, the USO made its telephone exchanges in Vietnam available to servicemen and women, enabling them to make as many as twenty-four thousand calls per month to loved ones in the United States. Another such program, known as Homecoming USA, operated from December 1970 to January 1972. It provided GIs with limited leave time and a way to fly back for brief stateside visits on inexpensive charter flights.

The Vietnam War challenged the USO's stateside operations as well. In the years after Korea through the early 1960s, public apathy to the conditions of military personnel had been a problem; after 1965, the unpopularity of the Vietnam War at home fostered much overt animosity toward armed forces personnel. Nonetheless, USO operations in the United States continued to attract volunteers, especially near major troop embarkation points, such as Oakland, California. Barbara J. Free, a volunteer at the USO in Oakland from 1966 to 1969, later described the experience:

> The Oakland USO had more than dances. Activities such as ping pong tournaments, picnics, [and] dance revues were planned around ship movements. I learned to make friends and say good-bye without crying in public. . . . My biggest USO thrill was not meeting Bob Hope at the national convention. It was giving support to the servicemen and women who during the Vietnam War got so little from the American public.

USO operations worldwide continued throughout the Vietnam War years. In 1967 a USO was opened on Malta for sailors of the Sixth Fleet serving in the eastern Mediterranean. Local USO operations were also maintained in the United States for soldiers in transit at airports in San Francisco and in Columbus, Ohio. The USO in Jacksonville, North Carolina, for service personnel stationed at nearby Camp Lejeune, was a particularly popular stateside USO facility during the war years.

In 1972, with the United States turning to a policy of "Vietnamization," which meant withdrawal of most U.S. forces, all USO facilities in Vietnam were closed. That year, Bob Hope gave his final USO Christmas Show at sites in Vietnam and Thailand. When asked once why he spent so many Christmases away from home, Hope replied, "I guess I got hooked on box lunches."

In a more serious vein, Hope managed to express the terrible dilemma that U.S. men and women who served in Vietnam—the most unpopular war in the nation's history—were forced to experience.

In Vietnam they were so grateful to you for coming they were fantastic. The last year [1972] we went there was the year that some anti-Vietnam newspapers criticized us for even going, but that was when the kids really needed us. There was a peace in the offing. They were waiting to go home and it didn't happen. It staggered them. Those poor guys were sitting over there with unopened champagne bottles. *That was when they needed the show more than anything else.*

The Vietnam War was one of the most harrowing, horrific, frustrating situations this nation's military has ever faced. The needs of the young men and women involved were enormous, as were the challenges for those who wanted to help them. The USO rose brilliantly to that special challenge, making the Vietnam era truly one of the organization's finest hours.

Another Hope "road to" picture; presumably the ladies will make the journey a short one. That's Jerry Colonna in the Santa suit.

American beauties. A San Francisco USO show, 1960.

Country and western legends Roy Rogers and Dale Evans were among the first entertainers to visit Vietnam, 1960.

Vietnam — it would only get worse.

The police action in Korea ended, but Hope's visits didn't. "Bayonet Bowl," Christmas 1962.

Danny Kaye is greeted by Capt. John Heath (left) and Capt. Rollin Westholm at Yokosuka Naval Base. Kaye was preparing a New Year's Day show, 1962.

Marine Cpl. Kenneth Coty found time to participate as a USO volunteer at Camp Lejeune, North Carolina, 1963.

The New York Times.

VOL. CXIII—No. 38,910.   © 1964 by The New York Times Company. Times Square, New York, N. Y. 10036   NEW YORK, WEDNESDAY, AUGUST 5, 1964.   TEN CENTS

U.S. PLANES ATTACK NORTH VIETNAM BASES; PRESIDENT ORDERS 'LIMITED' RETALIATION AFTER COMMUNISTS' PT BOATS RENEW RAIDS

F. B. I. Finds 3 Bodies Believed to Be Rights Workers'

GRAVES AT A DAM

Discovery Is Made in New Earth Mound in Mississippi

By CLAUDE SITTON
Special to The New York Times

JACKSON, Miss., Aug. 4—Bodies believed to be those of three civil rights workers missing since June 21 were found early tonight near Philadelphia, Miss.

Federal Bureau of Investigation agents recovered the bodies from a newly erected earthen dam in a thickly wooded area about six miles southwest of

Scattered Violence Keeps Jersey City Tense 3d Night

400 Policemen Confine Most of Rioters to 2 Sections—Crowds Watch in Streets Despite Danger

By FRED POWLEDGE
Special to The New York Times

JERSEY CITY, Aug. 4—Scattered violence broke out again here tonight as roving groups of Negroes hurled crude Molotov cocktails in the streets. There was some gunfire but no injuries were reported.

About 400 city policemen contained most of the young riot-

On Ocean Avenue the police trained spotlights on the roof of a three-story block of apartments. A man had been seen on the roof, and it was feared that he was armed with a rifle, fire bombs, or both. Yet on the sidewalk below, a woman walked her dog, apparently without concern, through throngs of hel-

REDS DRIVEN OFF

Two Torpedo Vessels Believed Sunk in Gulf of Tonkin

By ARNOLD H. LUBASCH
Special to The New York Times

WASHINGTON, Aug. 4—The Defense Department announced tonight that North Vietnamese PT boats made a "deliberate attack" today on two United States destroyers patrolling international waters in the Gulf of Tonkin off North Vietnam.

The attack came two days after North Vietnamese torpedo boats attacked the Maddox, one

2 CARRIERS USED

McNamara Reports on Aerial Strikes and Reinforcements

By JACK RAYMOND
Special to The New York Times

WASHINGTON, Wednesday, Aug. 5 — Secretary of Defense Robert S. McNamara said at a postmidnight news conference that the United States planes that attacked North Vietnam yesterday and today had come from the carriers Constellation and Ticonderoga in the Gulf of Tonkin.

FORCES ENLARGED

Stevenson to Appeal for Action by U.N. on 'Open Aggression'

By TOM WICKER
Special to The New York Times

WASHINGTON, Aug. 4—President Johnson has ordered retaliatory action against gunboats and "certain supporting facilities in North Vietnam" after renewed attacks against American destroyers in the Gulf of Tonkin.

In a television address tonight, Mr. Johnson said air attacks on the North Vietnamese ships and

The front page of the *New York Times*, August 5, 1964, the day after the Gulf of Tonkin incident, which began the escalation of U.S. involvement in Vietnam.

Arthur Godfrey strums his famous trademark, the ukulele, in Saigon, 1966.

A phone call home — it's only everything.

During his 1966 Christmas Show in Da Nang, Bob Hope introduced Gen. Emmett O'Donnell, Jr., USAF (Ret.), USO president from 1964 to 1971.

In the air over Southeast Asia: helicopters and machine guns.

President Lyndon Johnson flanked by Chairman Nguyen Van Thieu (left) and Prime Minister Nguyen Cau Ky of the Republic of South Vietnam in March 1967.

The USO Hollywood Overseas Committee brought Jonathan Winters to Vietnam in 1967. Then he brought the house down.

Classic Hope in Vietnam.

Phyllis Diller was a frequent Hope sidekick in Vietnam.

In 1967 Hollywood Overseas Committee chairman George Chandler (left) presents Governor Ronald Reagan with a plaque naming him honorary chairman of the California State USO.

"Gentlemen, start your engines!" Courtesy of the USO, service personnel's sons get ready for the European Soapbox 500.

USO Da Nang . . . the music flowed.

These boots are made for . . . boogying. Nancy Sinatra makes one soldier's day in Vietnam, 1967.

"There you go, soldier." A USO volunteer dispenses a Pepsi and a smile to a rain-soaked GI.

Americans in Paris with a view of one of the world's great symbols of freedom: the Arc de Triomphe.

Down to the sea in boats: a sailor's farewell to his family.

On steady sealegs, Bob Hope entertains sailors of the aircraft carrier USS *Bennington* off the coast of Vietnam, 1969.

Playing games on a USO-sponsored tour of Vietnam, all-star Wes Unseld of the Baltimore Bullets shows Lt. (jg) James Chadwick how it's done.

The indefatigable Martha Raye, one of the USO's greatest friends, flashes her famous smile.

Martha Raye, already wounded once in-country, returns to Vietnam as the star of *Hello Dolly*. Greeting her is Patricia Krause, director of Public Information, USO-Vietnam.

Put yourself in his boots. Without the USO this soldier, like thousands of others, would truly be alone in the crowd.

Steadfast, loyal, and funny, comedian George Gobel was a regular USO volunteer.

Seoul Rock: nine hours of music, five bands, and two thousand cups of coffee.

The late, great bandleader Xavier Cugat aboard the USS *Guadalcanal* off the Vietnam coast in 1967.

Patty and Maxene Andrews strutting their stuff in the USO-inspired musical, *Over Here!*

A warm Alaska welcome for Danny Kaye is posted on this Kuma Station quonset hut.

Jonathan warms 'em up. Winters in Vietnam, 1967.

Sailor D. T. Fannigan greets comedian George Jessel at the U.S. Naval Station, Norfolk, Virginia. Jessel was en route to a USO Pacific hospital tour.

If you've got to be away, the French Riviera isn't a bad place to be. And, of course, the USO is there to help out.

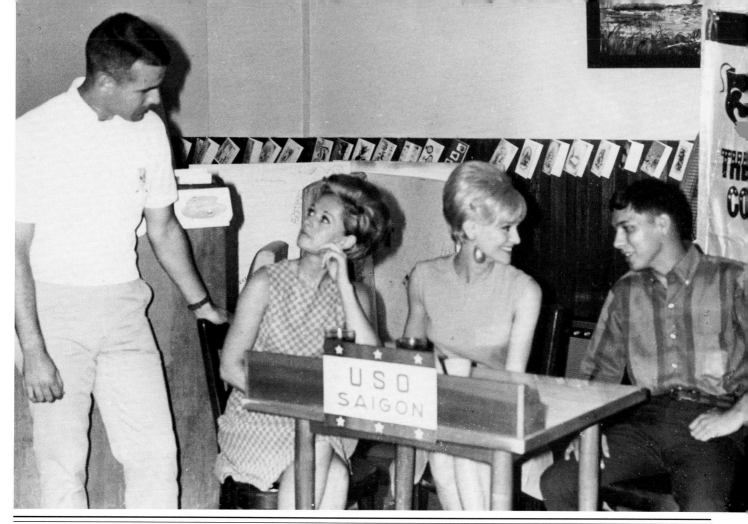

Actresses Tippi Hedren (left) and Diane McBain brighten up the 1967 Christmas holidays for a couple of GIs.

Sugar Ray Robinson, champion boxer and "class act," helped the USO provide special holiday telephone calls home for overseas service personnel.

Tennis anyone? Champions Gussie Moran and Nancy Chaffee Kiner brightened the Vietnam landscape during their 1970 tour.

Actor George Peppard, a former marine, visits a fire support base manned by the 1st Air Cav Division, 1970.

Heavyweight champ Floyd Patterson visits with servicemen in Vietnam.

The Duke, John Wayne, surrounded by admirers in Vietnam.

Wayne visiting a bivouac area in what soldiers called "the boonies."

A touch of home: servicemen and guests dance the night away at a USO club.

The USO facility in Chu Lai (I Corps) on the South China Sea. The I Corps region, which extended to the demilitarized zone (DMZ) and North Vietnam, and contained both Khe Sanh and My Lai, saw more than its share of tragedy.

A Jewish religious service in Saigon.

In the midst of war, a soldier prepares for a very special, peaceful day.

The Miss America tour, with Phyllis George up and strutting her stuff, visits the 101st Airborne in Vietnam, 1971.

A young Johnny Bench, now enshrined in baseball's Hall of Fame, visited Korea with Bob Hope during 1971's holiday season.

Actor Fess Parker visited fifteen USO Vietnam facilities during Christmas 1971.

Parker lends his shoulders to an ornament-wielding GI. The Christmas tree was one of three hundred provided to the troops during the 1971 holiday season.

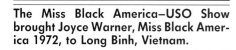

The Miss Black America–USO Show brought Joyce Warner, Miss Black America 1972, to Long Binh, Vietnam.

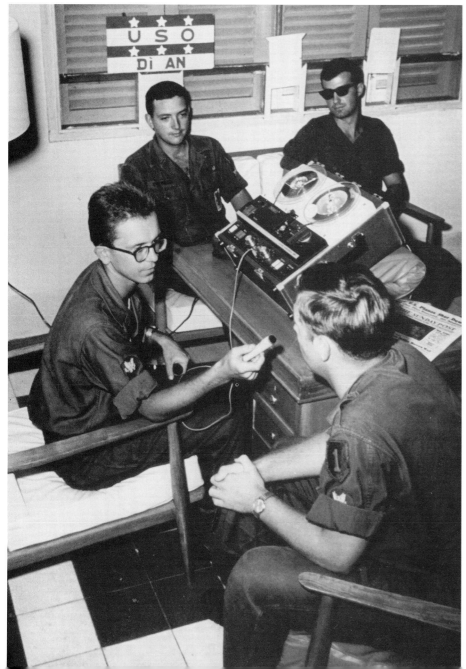

Tape recording a message home, thanks to the USO.

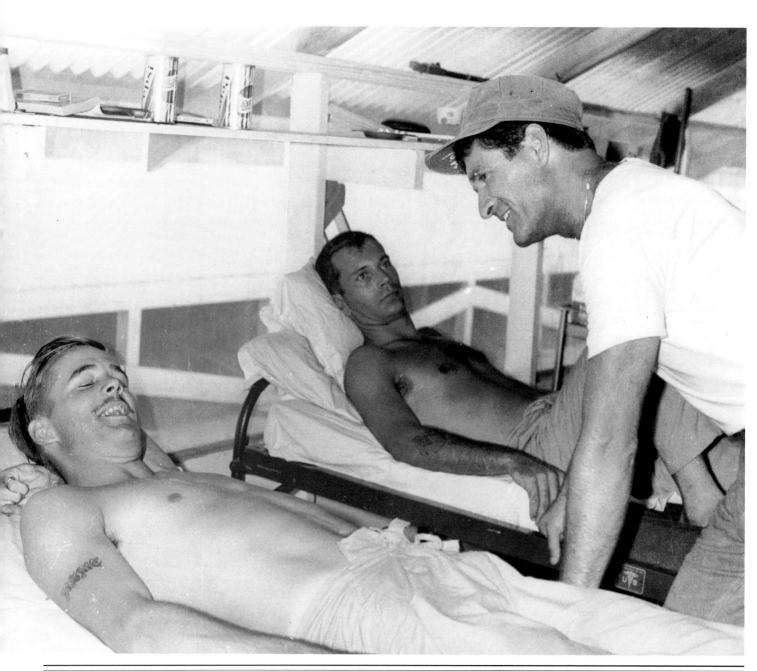

Hugh O'Brian visits wounded soldiers Cpl. John Vickers (left) and Sgt. L. N. Parks in Da Nang hospital prior to the USO–Hollywood Overseas Committee production of *Guys and Dolls*.

The late Sammy Davis, Jr. . . . over the years, a dedicated, ardent volunteer for the USO.

Henry Fonda being interviewed for Armed Forces Radio by program director Sgt. Dan Doherty.

In Vietnam. When Davis returned from his thirteen-base tour, he called it "one of the most exciting and satisfying experiences of my career."

Sebastian Cabot amused these patients on a USO tour.

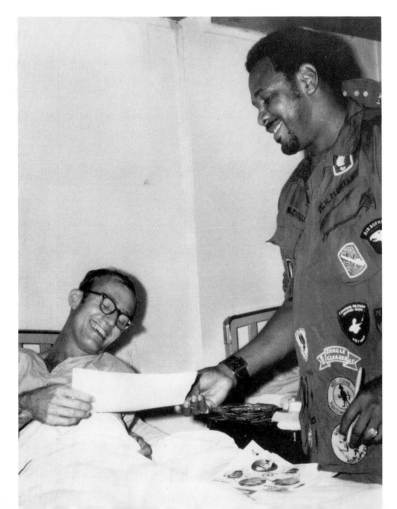

On a USO-sponsored tour, Pittsburgh Pirate slugger Willie Stargell's autograph brings a smile to this hospitalized soldier at Cam Ranh Bay, Vietnam.

A soldier relaxes under a USO tent.

The New York Times

LATE CITY EDITION
Weather: Rain late today, tonight becoming light snow early tomorrow. Temp. range: today 40-45; Saturday 40-44. Full U.S. report on Page 59.

SECTION ONE

VOL. CXXII .. No. 42,008   © 1973 The New York Times Company   NEW YORK, SUNDAY, JANUARY 28, 1973   25c beyond 50-mile zone from New York City, except Long Island. Higher in air delivery cities.   50 CENTS

VIETNAM PEACE PACTS SIGNED; AMERICA'S LONGEST WAR HALTS

Nation Ends Draft, Turns to Volunteers

Change Is Ordered Six Months Early— Youths Must Still Register

By DAVID E. ROSENBAUM
Special to The New York Times

WASHINGTON, Jan. 27—Defense Secretary Melvin R. Laird announced today that the military draft had ended.

As a result of the announcement, men born in 1953 and afterward will not be subject to conscription, and men born before 1953 but not yet drafted will have no further liability to the draft.

These men will be the first in two generations to have no prospect of being drafted. Except for a brief hiatus in 1947 and 1948, men have been conscripted regularly since 1940. President Nixon's authority the draft when they turn 18, and young men will still be assigned lottery numbers based on their birthdays.

Congress has mandated, however, that the Government call up Reserves and National Guardsmen before it turns to a reinstatement of the draft to meet future emergencies.

A spokesman for the Selective Service System said that men who had refused to report for induction would still be subject to criminal prosecution. But, he said, men with induction postponements that were due to expire before June

In the morning ceremony at the Hotel Majestic in Paris were, from the left, the Vietcong, North Vietnamese, South Vietnamese and U.S. delegations

CEREMONIES COOL

Two Sessions in Paris Formally Conclude the Agreement

By FLORA LEWIS
Special to The New York Times

PARIS, Jan. 27—The Vietnam cease-fire agreement was signed here today in eerie silence, without a word or a gesture to express the world's relief that the years of war were officially ending.

The accord was effective at 7 P.M. Eastern standard time.

Secretary of State William P. Rogers wrote his name 62 times on the documents providing—after 12 years—a settlement of the longest, most divisive foreign war in America's history.

The official title of the text was "Agreement on Ending the War and Restoring Peace in Vietnam." But the cold, almost

---

On January 28, 1973, peace in Vietnam is announced. It would, however, take more than two years before the last American troops would finally leave.

A man among men, Clint Eastwood visits the military.

One tradition that everyone can agree on: welcoming the fleet.

Chapter 8

After Vietnam: The USO and the All-Volunteer Armed Forces from the 1970s to the 1990s

The end of U.S. involvement in the Vietnam conflict marked the beginning of another lull in public support for the USO.

The unpopularity of the Vietnam War caused a rift between the military and civilian communities. And with the military's rapid transformation into an all-volunteer force, the United Way—the USO's major source of funding in the early 1970s—again questioned whether the USO was still needed. It was even suggested that since the new all-volunteer force was better paid, it no longer had to rely on the subsidized recreational opportunities the USO had traditionally provided.

In 1973 and 1974, a Blue Ribbon Study Committee was jointly commissioned by the United Way and the Department of Defense to determine if the USO had become obsolete in the face of the changes brought about by the all-volunteer armed forces. After having toured USO facilities both in the United States and overseas, the committee ultimately concluded that "if there were no USO, another organization would have to be created [to replace it]. . . . Isolation of the military from civilian influences is not, we believe, in the interest of this nation."

With this endorsement, the USO reemerged in the early 1970s with its aims adapted to meet the changes in the military population.

As the United States scaled down its military presence in Southeast Asia, the USO was able to concentrate its efforts on behalf of American service personnel in other parts of the world. Facilities were enlarged in Okinawa, Japan, and at airports in Atlanta, Honolulu, and Korea. In 1970 in Frankfurt, Germany, a major USO center was opened to meet the needs of U.S. servicemen and women and their families. (By 1990 there were eight USO centers in major German metropolitan cities with numerous satellite facilities throughout the country.)

The social needs of the all-volunteer forces were different from those of their predecessors in the World War II, Korea, and Vietnam eras. About half of the military personnel were married and had small children. USO Family and Community Centers began offering parenting and budgeting classes, forming family support groups, and providing recreational programs. (The trend toward

"Sailor, tuck in that shirt!" Don Knotts and "Admiral" Bob Hope.

family programs continued. Today's two million service members, while significantly younger than previous service generations—50 percent are below the age of twenty-five—have nearly three million spouses and children.)

In 1973 domestic USO affiliates began setting up satellite offices in civilian communities near U.S. military installations to help military families cope with housing and other social and economic problems. One such facility was at Bellevue, a federal housing project in Virginia, near Washington, D.C., where many Navy families lived.

Overseas, the USO began outreach programs for military families, providing family support groups, language courses, and other assistance needed by young families adapting to life in a foreign land.

With the armed forces having become more and more a "family affair," the USO adjusted to dealing with stresses unique to military family life. Because military families moved on an average of once every two years, services to those in transit became a priority for the USO in the 1970s. Travel assistance facilities were established at civilian and military airports in Europe and in the United States, and the USO also provided help in finding suitable off-base housing for relocated dependents of armed forces personnel. USO orientation and intercultural programs were started to help military families make a successful transition to life in a new country. In 1971 in Seoul, Korea, the USO created a "Brides School" to help Korean women who married Americans cope with the enormous cultural differences they would face when they settled in the United States.

Another big change that the USO had to address in the 1970s was the increased role of women in the armed forces. At its facilities in the United States and abroad, the USO established women's resource centers, places for female military personnel and military wives to meet and to exchange information.

The aim of all these programs was to assist service personnel in their involvement in the civilian community, and to aid them with a variety of complex situations such as housing, finances, and childcare, thereby enabling them to concentrate more effectively on carrying out their jobs in the military.

In the 1970s, the USO also stepped up its efforts to provide social and other support services to the increasing number of minorities, especially African Americans, making the military a career choice. With discrimination still present in some off-base communities in the Unites States, the USO became a leader in assuring equal treatment for all servicemen and women in their off-duty lives, no matter what their ethnic heritage.

In 1971 the USO began a counseling program for servicemen and women leaving the military, assisting them in obtaining educational opportunities and in dealing with other personal issues arising from the transition to civilian life.

After Vietnam, the USO continued to send show tours to U.S. bases overseas. On Veterans Day 1973, recognizing that veterans face emotional and psychological problems that cannot always be treated with medicine, the USO began sending its shows to veterans and military hospitals on a regular basis—a program that was to last for nearly ten years.

Throughout the 1970s, USO shows provided a wide variety of entertainment for armed forces personnel worldwide and for patients at military and veterans hospitals. Regulars on these show tours included the winner of the Miss America Pageant, star players from the National Football League, leading professional baseball players, and of course, the irrepressible Bob Hope, who regularly appeared at Veterans Administration (VA) hospitals, military bases, and on naval vessels. In addition, the USO brought dramatic productions from colleges and universities to stateside VA hospitals, as well as to U.S. military installations worldwide.

In 1977 the USO moved its headquarters from New York to Washington, D.C., a step that underscored the organization's role as a national agency serving the armed forces. By 1979 the six constituent agencies that had created the USO in 1941 withdrew, leaving the organization totally independent and self-directed. On December 20, 1979, by an act of Congress, the USO was granted a charter by the federal government, a step that brought much prestige and generated increased funding through the United Way, as well as through private donations from individuals and corporations. On May 30, 1985, the organization opened the Bob Hope USO Center and World Headquarters in Washington, D.C.

As the 1980s began, however, there were problems as well, particularly with the celebrity entertainment program that, after the end of the Vietnam conflict, had become virtually moribund. Few entertainers made themselves available to the USO, very likely a reaction to the fractious political debate over the U.S. involvement in Southeast Asia. Momentum had to be regained; somehow volunteering for the USO had to be again brought to the attention of those in the entertainment industry.

And once again the William Morris Agency, which under the aegis of Abe Lastfogel had been so instrumental in arranging the Hollywood community's contribution to the USO's efforts during World War II, would play an important role. Working under Lastfogel in the 1940s (in the mailroom) was a young man named Norman Brokaw, who in the ensuing years was to rise to the agency's leadership. His sons Sandy and David followed their father into the entertainment business. In September 1982 David Brokaw arranged for Lou Rawls, whom he represented, to tour military bases in the Pacific for the USO. The trip was a tremendous success—for the troops, for Rawls, and for the USO. The publicity the USO received was invaluable as once again the public—and entertainers—began to associate the USO with celebrities. Brokaw, who, by traveling with Lou Rawls, had experienced the unique emotional impact of a USO tour, immediately contacted David Skepner, manager for another Brokaw client, Loretta Lynn. She toured extensively in Europe during the Thanksgiving holidays of 1983. The trip was another success. The momentum had begun.

Other celebrities became interested in helping the USO. For example, the cast of the television hit *Happy Days* traveled to Europe for three consecutive years. The connection between the show and the USO was another bit of serendipity. One of the stars, Anson Williams ("Potsie"), was married to cast member Lorrie Mahaffey, daughter of Army Gen. Fred Mahaffey, who was stationed in Germany at the time. Williams saw for himself the difficulty of overseas duty; he returned to the States and enlisted fellow cast members, including Ron Howard, Henry Winkler, Pat Morita, and Marion Ross, for subsequent European and Pacific tours.

As the 1980s unfolded, the scene of international tension shifted to the Middle East, where the USO directed its efforts on behalf of U.S. service personnel stationed in the eastern Mediterranean. The USO's mobile Fleet Centers met ships at liberty ports to provide recreation and social support for thousands of Navy men and women.

In 1983 Bob Hope brought his USO show to the sailors and marines off the coast of Lebanon, with a special Christmas production that featured Vic Damone, Cathy Lee Cosby, George Kirby, Ann Jillian, Brooke Shields, and Miss USA, Julie Hyek. Others who visited troops stationed near Beirut that year were Charlton Heston, Wayne Newton, and Loretta Lynn. In fact, Lynn extended her originally scheduled tour after the Beirut bombing

occurred and became the first entertainer to visit troops around Beirut after that tragedy.

In 1984 a major USO center opened in Haifa, Israel, while USO centers at bases in Europe, the Caribbean, the South Pacific, and the Far East continued to provide recreational and support programs for U.S. service personnel and their families. In addition to providing traditional USO services in fleet, airport, and family centers for stateside military families, the USO became a referral agency to outside social welfare programs and carried on family outreach programs and self-help groups.

In 1984 rock musicians started to get involved too. Phil Ehart, founder and drummer for the rock group KANSAS, put together a group of all-star musicians from the Doobie Brothers; Crosby, Stills & Nash; Cheap Trick; and Pablo Cruise as well as KANSAS to tour for the USO.

In three annual tours that followed Ehart's efforts, the "USO's 1st Airborne Rock-n-Roll Division" would perform at American bases in Japan, Okinawa, the Philippines, Hawaii, the Indian Ocean, the eastern Mediterranean, Germany, Greece, Italy, Spain, Portugal, and at domestic USO fund-raising concerts in San Diego and Baton Rouge.

Aboard the USS *Eisenhower* off the coast of Libya, Stephen Stills was asked, "Why are you here?" He answered:

> This is something that I've been wanting to do for a long time. You know, we're Americans, and we get to agree or disagree . . . with policy decisions. But that doesn't matter. The soldiers are just out here, and they don't know anything about all of that. They're here, and I wanted to come and say thanks for being here. The *Eisenhower* isn't going to get back to port for yet another forty days, so they got our show. So, it's crucial, I think.

Also joining the overseas circuit in the late 1980s were the Charlie Daniels Band; Mickey Gilley; Earth, Wind & Fire; and Atlantic Starr, as well as Miss USA. Popular country and western stars also did their part for the USO in the 1980s, with Randy Travis, the mother-daughter team of Naomi and Wynonna Judd (The Judds), Ricky Skaggs, Charley Pride, and Lee Greenwood leading the way. The Nashville Network (TNN) aired a series of the USO country music tours from 1986 to 1989.

Still proud. The USO Club in Jacksonville, North Carolina.

In 1987, when the U.S. Navy was deployed in the Persian Gulf to protect reflagged Kuwaiti tankers, the USO sent Bob Hope, Lee Greenwood, Barbara Eden, Connie Stevens, Pearl Bailey, and Wayne Newton to entertain the sailors on U.S. ships in the region. Others who toured that year for the USO were Randy Travis; "Jeopardy!" host Alex Trebek, who conducts contestant searches on military bases; and the Dallas Cowboys Cheerleaders, who started touring for the USO in 1979 and have toured twice annually since.

In 1987, under the terms of a new Memorandum of Understanding with the Department of Defense, the USO was recognized as the principal channel representing civilian concern for the U.S. armed forces worldwide.

Although U.S. troops overseas in the 1980s generally did not face combat conditions, there was always the threat of terrorism. On April 14, 1988, a terrorist car bomb exploded outside the USO Fleet Center in Naples, Italy, destroying the center and killing five people. Among the dead was Petty Officer Angela Simone Santos, twenty-two years old, the first woman in the U.S. Navy to die in a terrorist attack.

Just hours before the U.S. invasion of Panama in late 1989, country and western music superstar Charley Pride played for American forces in the Canal Zone.

In the Philippines in 1989, when rising political tensions coupled with terrorist attacks on U.S. servicemen stationed there caused all liberty and leave to be canceled, the USO stepped up its efforts to provide recreation and support for the thousands of military personnel who found themselves confined to base. In January 1991, just a month before the USO's fiftieth anniversary, "Piano Man" Billy Joel performed two concerts at Subic Bay Naval Base and Clark Air Base for the Americans doing difficult duty in the Philippines.

In 1990 José Feliciano played at U.S. military installations in South Korea. Also that year, Bob Hope, with comedian Yakov Smirnoff, singer Rosemary Clooney, LaToya Jackson, Miss Universe, and Brooke Shields played for American military personnel in Frankfurt, Germany, and Cambridge, England. They also performed in Moscow for American embassy civilian staffers, marine guards, and Soviet guests.

On August 2, 1990, Iraq's invasion of Kuwait led to a massive buildup of U.S. armed forces in Saudi Arabia and the Persian Gulf. Within weeks, several hundred thousand American military personnel were deployed to Saudi Arabia and on ships in the Persian Gulf, not knowing how long they would be there or if the crisis would erupt into an actual shooting war. With its traditional promptness, the USO immediately rose to the occasion, opening Fleet Centers in the Persian Gulf ports of Dubai and Bahrain, while providing stateside support for the spouses of service personnel, both reservists and regulars, who had suddenly been called away on active duty.

With Operation Desert Shield affecting every U.S. military facility in the world, virtually all USO centers had to respond accordingly. "Tent cities" began popping up around the world to shelter servicemen and women transiting to the Middle East — and the USO responded. For example, since day one of the Saudi deployment, the USO in Frankfurt, Germany, has had a 24-hour presence in "Tent City" at Rhein Main Air Base.

In October 1990 comedian Steve Martin and his wife, actress Victoria Tennant, visited the troops in Saudi Arabia on a personal appearance tour for the USO. Commenting on the Steve Martin visit, Kevin McCarthy, executive producer for the USO, said,

> We visited the troops all the way out at the front lines: It was seven days of the toughest travel and working conditions I've seen in ten years of producing USO tours. But it was well worth it. . . . Steve and Victoria were complete "troopers," and their visit was a terrific boost to men and women facing serious, deadly conflict.

Martin was followed by boxing champion Thomas Hearns and then, over Thanksgiving 1990, by comedian Jay Leno. All these celebrities volunteered their talents for shows to U.S. service personnel deployed in the Persian Gulf, with the tours' expenses paid for by a $2.5 million Gulf Crisis Fund provided by contributions from the Coca-Cola Company, ARCO, American International Group (AIG), Anheuser-Busch, and AT&T. Hollywood also did its part by providing video cassettes of newly released motion pictures.

Other morale efforts were put into action, including a call for Americans to write letters to servicemen and women to show that they had the support of the people back home. More dramatic was the USO's "Better Than A Letter" program begun by Montgomery Ward chairman Bernard Brennan. By Christmas 1990 the program had provided over 450 camcorders, 400 VCRs and televisions, and over a quarter million blank tapes to the troops in Saudi Arabia, allowing virtually every serviceman and woman deployed for Operation Desert Shield the opportunity to send a videotaped recording to their families. In addition, every Montgomery Ward store in the United States provided viewing and recording facilities for family members.

The challenges were new in the 1970s and 1980s. The USO responded, particularly with the resurrection of the celebrity entertainment program, growing and adapting to meet the changing needs of a new generation of American military personnel and their families.

Young servicemen enjoying themselves. Isn't this what the USO is all about? Jacksonville, North Carolina, Christmas 1983.

Basketball legend Marques Haynes (second from left) took his Harlem Wizards to Europe for the USO in 1982.

During the USO's fortieth anniversary year, Walt Disney World provided special discounts for members of the armed forces and their families.

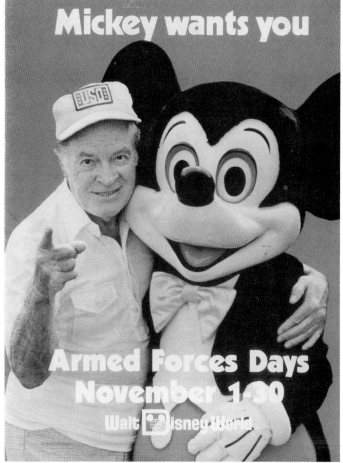

At the USO's Presidential Salute in October 1981, President Ronald Reagan and former-President Gerald Ford flank outranked comedian Hope.

What's the USO? It's entertainment and a welcome break from monotony at remote bases overseas. No one's done it better than Bob Hope. President Reagan congratulates the comedian on a lifetime of service.

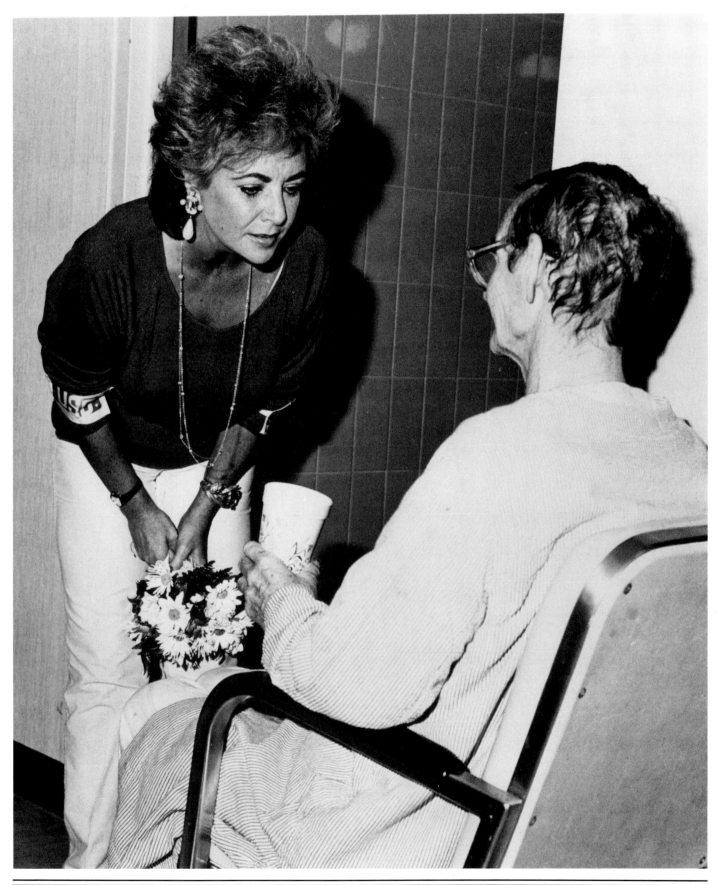

Elizabeth Taylor visits a hospitalized vet.

Country and western singing legend Loretta Lynn has been a regular USO volunteer since the early 1980s.

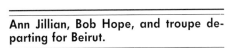

Ann Jillian, Bob Hope, and troupe departing for Beirut.

The Bob Hope Christmas Show in Beirut, 1983, shortly after the tragic bombing of the U.S. Marine barracks. Left to right: Vic Damone, Brooke Shields, Cathy Lee Crosby, Hope, Miss USA, George Kirby, and Ann Jillian.

Singer Randy Travis can always be counted on when the USO calls.

Another regular on the USO circuit: Pearl Bailey at sea.

Liza Minelli, like her mother Judy Garland, has often helped the USO.

Kris Kristofferson, a West Point graduate, is another "regular" on the USO team.

Budweiser sponsored a USO fund-raising tour for the rock group Toto.

Hope and more Hope. Outside the Bob Hope USO Headquarters, the comedian "busses" a bust, his own.

Ronald Reagan speaks out for the "Volunteers of America," the USO.

In big towns and small, the USO is always home.

And he's still flying high. The Air Force Academy honored Hope on his seventy-seventh birthday.

Mickey Gilley and band on his tour to Diego Garcia, Indian Ocean, 1985.

The eyes of Texas are upon her. Brooke Shields has given freely of her time for the USO. Here she is with Doris Dixon at a forty-fifth USO anniversary dinner in Dallas.

An American classic.

In the Persian Gulf, singer Lee Greenwood entertains on the USS *Okinawa* during the USO's 1987 Christmas Show. The USO has had, over the years, few better friends than Greenwood.

Loretta Lynn takes off for the USO . . . again.

Then-Vice President and Mrs. George Bush greet the estimable Hope.

Randy Travis performing during the AT&T-sponsored USO tour
to the Middle East, 1990.

Country and western singer Ricky Skaggs has been especially
generous with his support for the USO.

The Reagan Friendship Flight, October 1989. The USO and the former president provided these families of military personnel stationed in Japan with free round-trip airfare to visit their loved ones.

The Dallas Cowboys Cheerleaders, who have toured twenty-one times for the USO, on a December 1989 Far East tour.

Earth, Wind & Fire on tour in Okinawa and Korea during November 1990.

Celebrities Miss Piggy and Kermit with mentors Frank Oz (left) and the wondrous Jim Henson.

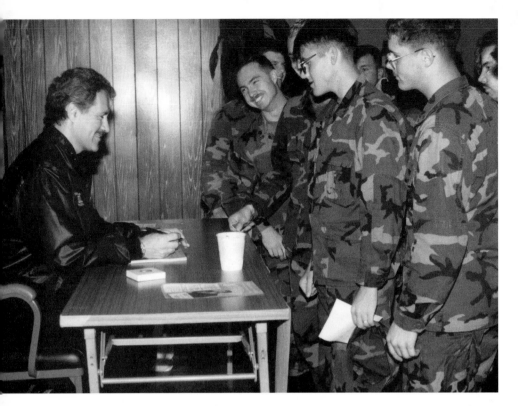

Alex Trebek of "Jeopardy!" on his 1990 European tour.

José Feliciano on tour in Korea, 1990.

Boxer Thomas Hearns visited Gen. Norman Schwarzkopf, commander in chief of U.S. Central Command, in Saudi Arabia, November 1990.

Jay Leno entertains the troops in Saudi Arabia, Thanksgiving 1990.

Hearns with troops serving in Operation Desert Shield.

Steve Martin with troops in Saudi Arabia.

Billy Joel, in "full tilt boogie," rocks out in his USO tour of the Philippines, January 1991.

"Piano Man" to "Rain Man": Despite a mid-concert deluge, Joel and band played on — to the delight of U.S. service personnel and their families.

Martin tries an MRE (Meal Ready to Eat); wife Victoria Tennant and soldier enjoy the action.

Steadfast and stalwart: Bob Hope during his 1990 Christmas USO tour to the Persian Gulf.

Television stars and marriage partners Delta Burke and Gerald McRaney outflank Gen. Norman Schwarzkopf during their USO-sponsored tour of Operation Desert Shield (1990).

U S O
A Family Affair

Chapter 9

Thanks for the Memories

The story of the USO's first half-century parallels the history of the United States as it emerged as an international superpower. As war threatened and erupted, the USO was there to keep up the morale of America's fighting forces, both overseas and abroad. For those young American men and women who had dedicated themselves to the difficult task of waging the peace, the USO was also there to make their job a little easier. As stated in 1989 by Charles T. ("Chuck") Hagel, then president of the USO and himself a twice-wounded and highly decorated Vietnam veteran:

> I don't know of a tougher job anywhere than being in the military. The uncertainty, always the threat of terrorism, always the danger and hardship. It's a tough job, and the USO provides at least some semblance of a "home away from home."

For fifty years the USO has meant a little bit of home in a faraway place. Where Americans have gone, the USO has gone. A private in the U.S. Army provided a succinct testimonial to the USO when he wrote in 1941: "Golly, it was good to have a bath. . . . We soldiers will be thankful for it the rest of our lives."

It can truly be said that the USO has represented the best in the American people — compassion, magnanimity, selflessness, service — universally admired qualities that the USO has mirrored to the world at large. For the generations of men and women it has served, the USO has meant friendship, respite, familiarity, warmth, and acceptance.

Inherent in the USO's mission is a simple faith that the world can be made a better place. "So long as we love," Robert Louis Stevenson wrote more than a hundred years ago, "we serve; so long as we are loved by others, we are indispensable."

To the USO on its fiftieth anniversary, . . . thanks for the memories.

Important Dates in USO History

February 4, 1941	The USO is incorporated under the laws of the state of New York.
October 30, 1941	USO establishes Camp Shows, Inc.
November 28, 1941	The first government-built USO club opens at Fayetteville, North Carolina.
December 31, 1947	All USO clubs and facilities are closed, and the organization is given an honorable discharge by President Harry S Truman.
January 1951	The USO is reactivated for the Korean War under a Memorandum of Understanding between the president and the Department of Defense.
1962–63	The Hannah Survey reaffirms the need for a peacetime USO.
September 1963	USO opens its first club in Saigon, Vietnam; seventeen others are established in Vietnam over the next nine years.
December 1964	Bob Hope makes his first Christmas Show tour of Vietnam.
June 1972	All USO clubs in Vietnam are closed as American troops withdraw.
1977	USO moves its World Headquarters from New York to Washington, D.C.
December 20, 1979	President Jimmy Carter signs the USO's newly granted congressional charter.
May 30, 1985	The Bob Hope USO Center and World Headquarters opens in Washington, D.C.
September–December 1990	The USO opens two centers in the Middle East in Bahrain and the United Arab Emirates.
February 4, 1991	The USO celebrates its fiftieth anniversary.

Credits

Unless otherwise noted below, all photos and art are courtesy of World USO.

Lisa Berg: 158 *bottom*

The *Cleveland News*: 8 *top*

Jack Douthitt: 168, 169

Neil Greentree: 160 *bottom*, 165, 166, 167

Jim Kenah: 162, 163, 164

Library of Congress: 8 *bottom*, 9 *top*, 16 *top*, 19 *top*

National Archives: 15 *top*, 32, 41, 42 *top*, 43, 44, 46, 47, 49, 55, 56, 57, 58, 66, 72, 73, 74–75, 76, 101

The New York Times Company: 12 *bottom*, 53, 99 *top*, 133 *top*

The Norman Rockwell Family Trust: 23

David Skepner: 160 *top*

About the Author

Frank Coffey, a former book and magazine editor, is the author of four novels as well as numerous magazine and newspaper pieces. The son of a decorated World War II B-26 pilot, he has had a lifelong interest in military history. Now a screenwriter and journalist, he lives in New York City.